in
visi
ble.

Jacqueline Leckie

in visi ble.

New Zealand's history of excluding Kiwi-Indians

Contents.

Forewords

It's really important to publish *Invisible: New Zealand's history of excluding Kiwi-Indians* at a time when Aotearoa is grappling with its history. Our schools have been mandated to teach the spectrum of New Zealand history from 2020, and the publication of this book will add to a rich tapestry, filling the gap in our collective knowledge of the experiences of Indian people in Aotearoa New Zealand.

Indian history in this land is complex and has been captured in great detail by Dr Leckie, from the time of Cook in 1769 to the present. Interactions between Indian individuals, families and communities with broader society have paralleled colonial history. There are the familiar patterns of exclusion and exploitation we see in so many spheres of our society, whether at the picture theatre in Pukekohe — which has earned a place in New Zealand history for racial exclusion, and for segregating the races — to immigration policies that officially welcomed all 'members of the empire', while quietly emulating the White Australia policy behind the scenes.

I'm impressed with the way that Dr Leckie has uncovered hundreds of case studies of the lives of Indian people in New Zealand. The way they have adapted, prospered, pushed back and gone about building their lives and communities in a strange land is inspiring.

I thank the New Zealand Indian Central Association for the invitation to introduce and to mihi to *Invisible*. After the Covid-19 lockdown, the Human Rights Commission launched the Voice of Racism campaign, which has, in a small way, captured the experiences of Indian New Zealanders. Being asked 'but where are you are *really* from?' is an example of repetitive questioning in the book that we captured in the campaign. It is my sincere hope that *Invisible* takes pride of place on the nation's bookshelves and in schools. I appreciate the role it will have in educating our people about racism and the real impacts it has on the lives of Indian New Zealanders. It should motivate us all to stand up to racism, the one aspect of New Zealand history we must banish to the past. In Aotearoa, diversity is our strength.

Meng Foon
Race Relations Commissioner
May 2021

I*nvisible: New Zealand's history of excluding Kiwi-Indians* is an exciting and galvanising book by Dr Jacqueline Leckie. It introduces readers to the hardships faced by Indians upon their arrival in Aotearoa New Zealand because of the colour of their skin and the way they spoke.

This book was instigated by the presentation of a Grievance Report by Naginbhai G. Patel of Wellington to the 79th NZICA Annual General Meeting, sixteen years ago, on 9 April 2005. It is from the revelations presented in that report that *Invisible* has been developed and published.

Dr Leckie has brought to life the experiences of early Indian settlers and the challenges they faced as people of a different ethnic background to the majority of new migrants. Although the first signs of racism were directed to new ethnic groups very early in New Zealand's history, racism against Indians and Chinese carried on for a number of years. It took the will of some determined early settlers to recognise this and make a stand by raising issues of discrimination with government authorities. However, positive outcomes from this would take many years.

Racism is unfortunately still amongst us, and *Invisible* also describes the experiences of Indian communities through to today. This racism is not only directed against the first ethnic settlers of non-European descent, such as Indians and Chinese, but now it is also directed towards other ethnic groups.

I would like to thank the various NZICA members, including a special mention to NZICA General Secretary Manisha Morar, for assisting Dr Leckie by providing information and photographs.

This invaluable work informs readers about an aspect of our history that is often hidden, provides a glimpse of the difficult experiences of early settlers and explores what ethnic racism is like in Aotearoa New Zealand today.

Paul Patel QSM
President New Zealand Indian Central Association Inc
May 2021

one.

The Indian Diaspora and Exclusion

On 15 March 2019 a white terrorist stormed into the Al Noor mosque in Christchurch and opened fire with a deadly arsenal of weapons, just as around 350 Muslims were about to begin Friday prayers. He then attacked worshippers at the city's Linwood Islamic Centre. A total of 51 people were killed and 49 injured. Before committing these atrocities, the attacker had posted his intentions online, along with a venomous manifesto. He then live-streamed the first massacre.

Kiwis and people worldwide reacted to the news with a range of emotions from shock and anger to empathy and love for the victims. Yet the outpouring of grief was overlaid by a collective denial that such evil lurked within the nation. True, the murderer was an Australian immigrant, but how could he commit such terrorism in peaceful and tolerant Aotearoa? Indeed, Prime Minister Jacinda Ardern declared that the person who committed the racist violence 'is not us'. When she said that Muslims 'have chosen to make New Zealand their home, and it is their home. They are us,' she could have been referring to any immigrants, including Indians. Ardern's condemnation of the unprecedented actions of 15 March may have been true in spirit, but that horror pointed to the presence of white extremism and tacit or unintentional support within Aotearoa. Within six months of the killings, the vice-chancellor of the University of Auckland allowed the distribution of white supremacist literature on campus on the grounds of freedom of speech.

The Christchurch massacre raised questions about what it means to belong to an ethnic and/or religious minority in a country that has experienced a very long history of underlying prejudice and racism. After all, New Zealand is founded upon colonialism, predicated by white racial domination. The concept of the nation and nationalism — which assumes a 'singular shared identity within it and denies difference outside its borders'[1] — has remained problematic in New Zealand. The Treaty of Waitangi Te Tiriti o Waitangi, signed in 1840, ostensibly represented a partnership between indigenous Māori and the British Crown, but it did not eliminate racism towards Māori or material and cultural loss, deprivation and marginalisation. The passing of the 1975 Treaty of Waitangi Act instigated a process of reparations and ushered in recognition of New Zealand as a bicultural nation — but, again, this did not see an end to racism.[2]

In the aftermath of the Christchurch massacre, clinical psychologist Waikaremoana Waitoki asked, 'Why did our country have to hit rock bottom and lose 50[3] lives before we asked ourselves to look inwards at the institutions that enabled racism to thrive? Alongside that introspection, did we look at our own actions, or inactions, that foster racism, not only towards Māori, but to anyone who was not Christian and Caucasian?'[4] Or as lawyer and Te Tiriti specialist Moana Jackson stressed, '[T]he massacres in Christchurch and the ideologies of racism and white supremacy which underpinned them did not come about in some non-contextual vacuum. They are instead a manifestation of the particular history of colonisation and its founding presumption that the so-called white people in Europe were inherently superior to everyone else.'[5]

But what of the experiences of non-European migrants, specifically Indians and their descendants, in Aotearoa? Both within the negative history of colonisation and racism and, more positively, within the scope of the Treaty and biculturalism?[6]

This book adds to the story of migration and belonging from the perspective of Indians in Aotearoa New Zealand. It seeks to uncover what Sir Anand Satyanand, a son of Indo-Fijian migrants and a former governor-general, termed the 'dark side of history'[7] and historian Sekhar Bandyopadhyay described as a 'story of exclusion' that renders Indians' existence 'invisible' in our narratives.[8] This disturbing history highlights negative and offensive white voices, but where possible it also reflects upon the pride of Kiwi-Indian migrants in their new homeland.[9] Unlike existing publications on Indians in New Zealand, this is not a history of celebration or integration, but speaks instead of stories of resilience, while also outlining the discrimination Kiwi-Indians have faced, so that all New Zealanders can recognise and address the nation's uncomfortable past. It can be tempting to dismiss past anti-Asian rhetoric as crackpot and belonging to a different time, but it is too easy to sweep this history under the carpet,[10] and to do the same with contemporary racism directed at Indians.

This book is not offered as a solution to persistent racism and discrimination. It does not address exclusion within Kiwi-Indian communities that may be based on caste, religion, status and gender, as well as economic exploitation.[11] The book does not explain 15 March 2019. Rather, it hopes to shed some light on how that tragedy could happen in a nation where the extreme outcome of racism 'is not us'. Aotearoa New Zealand's record of the exclusion of Kiwi-Indians is a legacy that challenges the nation's view of itself as inclusive and open.

Exclusion of Kiwi-Indians throughout New Zealand's history was sometimes overt, but more often less sensational and more insidious. The white New Zealand immigration policy was the first hurdle Indians faced when coming to New Zealand. Most Indians also encountered other forms of discrimination, often institutional, or racism embedded in social interactions that was more subtle and nebulous. In many instances the prejudice was colour- and race-based; a whites-only discourse where Indians were discriminated against along with all 'non-whites', including Māori. There was also widespread expression of an anti-Asian sentiment, and in New Zealand this mostly affected Indians and Chinese.[12]

Most liberal Kiwis condemn racism directed towards Asians, but the dominant perception associates this racism with the history of the Chinese in Aotearoa. Chinese faced widespread prejudice during the second half of the nineteenth century. The Chinese Immigrants Act 1881 levied an entry (or 'poll') tax of £10 on each Chinese immigrant, while ships arriving in New Zealand were restricted to one Chinese passenger per 10 tons of cargo. In 1896 this 'tonnage' ratio was reduced to one passenger for 200 tons of cargo, but the poll tax was increased to £100 (estimated to be $20,000 today). The First Labour Government abolished these provisions in 1944.[13] This discrimination was publicly acknowledged on 2 February 2002, when Prime Minister Helen Clark formally apologised to Chinese New Zealanders for the tonnage restriction and poll tax imposed on Chinese arrivals to Aotearoa.

Meanwhile, the history of discriminatory practices explicitly directed at Indians in Aotearoa New Zealand — and moreover the complex history of Indian settlement here — has tended either to have been invisible or just not discussed. Such neglect may not be intentional but speaks to national histories written either through a white lens or with a bicultural framework of Māori and Pākehā applied; perhaps with Indians hidden in the footnotes or subsumed within the generalised past and contemporary discourse about 'Asiatics' or Asians in Aotearoa.

A key reason for this discomfort and ambivalence concerning the rights of Indians in Aotearoa is that, although considered a different race and colour, the majority were, unlike the Chinese, subjects of the British Empire.[14] The pathways of Indian migration to Aotearoa were a consequence of British imperialism, formalised after 1857, on the exploitative foundations of the East India Company, which profoundly restructured economy, society and politics on the Indian subcontinent. Landlessness, indebtedness and other economic pressures induced outwards migration that invariably followed the sea routes by which Britain operated its empire. By the late nineteenth century Indian migrants also met common exclusionary policies and practices within British settler colonies where the Indian diaspora had begun to take root. This was despite Queen Victoria proclaiming to the 'Princes, Chiefs and People of India' that she would grant 'the Natives of Our Indian Territories' the same rights as 'all Our other Subjects' and, among other things, to support religious toleration, to recognise the 'Customs of India', to end racial discrimination and to ensure that 'all shall alike enjoy the equal impartial protection of the Law'.[15] By the 1920s Indians in New Zealand would regard Queen Victoria's promise of equality as null and void.

Still little known to most Kiwis is that Indians arrived in Aotearoa about the same time as Europeans and Māori first made contact on land. Todd Nachowitz has argued that it is crucial to unpack this erased history and participation of ethnic minorities within Aotearoa's history to 'help relevant minorities reclaim association in a newly formed shared national identity that has the potential to strengthen social cohesion'.[16] He suggests that embedding Indian history within that of Aotearoa, and its bicultural foundation, should highlight an Indian perspective. Although the details of very early Indian encounters in Aotearoa have been lost in time, it is important to put on record evidence of an early Indian presence on these shores. Indians may have been invisible within dominant historical narratives, but they are 'equally entitled to claim their place in the history of first encounter and the exploration and settlement of New Zealand'.[17]

The earliest Indian visitors to Aotearoa were Indian lascars (seamen) working on European ships. In 1769, 14-year-old 'Mamouth Cassem' (probably Mahmud Qāsim), born in Pondicherry, and a Bengali named 'Nasrin' (Nasreen), aged about 16 or 17, most probably came ashore when the *Saint Jean-Baptiste* berthed in the Hokianga during 12–31 December of that year. The ship was under the command of Captain Jean François Marie de Surville, who was conducting a Pacific trading voyage on behalf of the French East India Company.

From 1794 to 1801 trading ships of the British East India Company sailed between England, South Africa, India, Australia and China, and Aotearoa New Zealand was part of some of these routes. Indian lascars crewed these ships, and sepoys (Indian soldiers under British or other imperial orders) were also on board. Stops ashore in Aotearoa were made to collect supplies and seal skins and to cut timber. Some lascars were at Tamatea (Dusky Sound in Fiordland) between 1795 and 1797.

Indian sailors also 'jumped ship' and settled among Māori. Reasons for this would have included the attraction of a new life, and the desire to escape poor shipboard conditions and harsh treatment from Europeans.[18] In 1809, a Bengali deserted the ship *City of Edinburgh* to live with his Māori wife in the Bay of Islands.[19] In 1814, six Indian sailors stole a boat and left the *Matilda*, either on the south-west coast of the South Island or at Port Daniel (Otago Harbour) in 1814.[20] Three were killed but three survived, probably settling near Whareakeake in Otago until 1823. One survivor, probably from Surat, spoke English and Māori and was given the name Te Anu. Bishop Selwyn said the man was living with his Māori wife and son at Potirepo (Port William) on Rakiura (Stewart Island) in 1844.[21]

During the nineteenth century, Indians worked throughout Aotearoa — including Te Waipounamu (South Island) — more than is now recalled. Many were Muslims, such as 'Butterdean' (Badrudeen) from Kashmir, who was living in Otago in 1875.[22]

Other early Indian migrants were the Sohman (originally Somen) and Bussawan families. They were among 17 servants indentured to

John Sohman (formerly Somen) was one of the early migrants from India. He arrived in Canterbury in 1859 as an indentured servant. He later settled at Oxford and was a staunch supporter of the Salvation Army.

Edward Peters: Discovered gold, died a pauper

Until the unveiling by Governor-General Anand Satyanand of a memorial at Glenore, Otago, on Easter Saturday 2009, Edward Peters was erased from his rightful place in Aotearoa New Zealand's history as the discoverer of gold in the Tuapeka area of Otago in 1857. Peters — variously described as Eurasian, a 'half-caste', 'native of Bombay' and a Goan (he was born in Satara, Maharashtra, which is close to Goa) — left India to work on the California goldfields. He signed up as a cook on the sailing ship *Maori*, which left Gravesend in England in 1853. On 31 August 1853 Peters absconded after the ship had docked at Port Chalmers. He reported to the police and was sentenced to six weeks' hard labour, after which he was free to settle in Otago. He worked as a farm labourer and gold prospector in the Tokomairiro, Tuapeka and Molyneux districts, where he was called 'Black Peter' — indicative of how his identity was racialised. Peters was denied recognition as the discoverer of the source of the Otago gold rush, and instead the accolades went to Gabriel Read, who registered a claim in 1861. Read was awarded £1000 from the provincial government for the discovery, but Peters was denied any prize. Later, the Goldfields Committee launched an appeal which

The Story of Black Peter.

AN APPEAL.

There is a man living amongst us who may fairly claim to be the Father of Gold-mining in New Zealand. His name is Edward Peters, native of Bombay, better known, perhaps, as "Black Peter" by old residents. He was the first man to demonstrate, by actual discovery, the existence of payable gold-workings in Otago; but he was poor, humble, and ignorant, and did not know how to turn his discoveries to profitable account. Wherefore he has been neglected, and the value of his work has been ignored except by the few who are acquainted with the facts; and the honours and the rewards that should have been his have been awarded to others.

Otago Witness, 5 December 1885

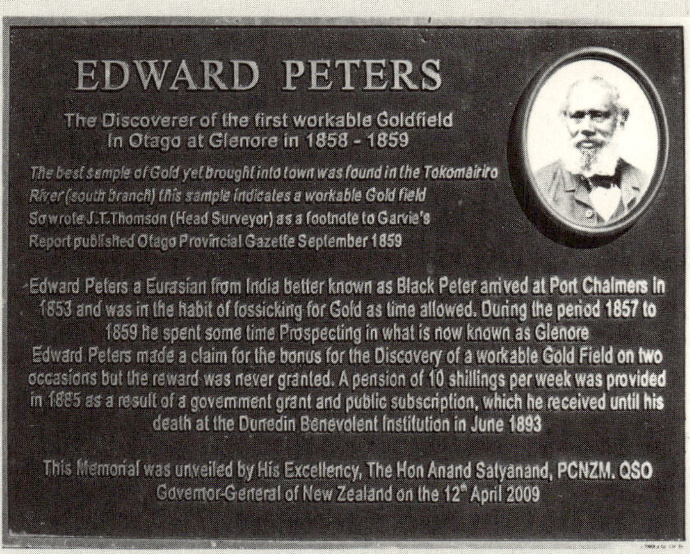

A memorial plaque dedicated to Edward Peters was unveiled in 2009. His discovery of gold began the Otago gold rush, but this was never officially recognised. Instead the reward and fame went to Gabriel Read.

granted Peters an allowance of 10 shillings a week. Peters was aged in his sixties when he died in 1893 as a pauper in Dunedin's Benevolent Institution. But he left behind friends who vowed that his contribution to Otago's history should not be erased. Mrs C. R. Mitchell of Balclutha wrote in Peters' obituary that 'Peter would have been above the average class of people one meets with in everyday life. He was always gentle and kindly to animals, and very tender over young children. How he first discovered gold in Otago is well known to the reading public; also how another won the renown and reward that should have been his. "Black Peter" another of our pioneers has passed away, and his name must ever be associated with the early history of Otago.' [23]

Stories about Peters continued to be passed down within local families, and in 2009, farmer and historian Alan Williams and the Glenore Manuka Trust finally made sure that Peters was commemorated. So, too, did Edward Ellison, a kaumātua of Te Rūnaka o Ōtākou. Williams suggests that Peters was a victim of local politics as he was not part of the powerful social networks in which Read very likely participated.[24]

work on the Cashmere Estate at Christchurch in 1859 by a former judge in India, Sir John Cracroft Wilson. These Indians and their descendants either died or married Māori and Europeans.[25] John Sohman and his family settled in Oxford, north of Christchurch, where he and his daughter were active within the Salvation Army. We will return to John's story later in the book, when the Registrar of Pensions tried to cancel his old-age pension in 1907.

By the late nineteenth century the roots of New Zealand's Indian community were laid when chain migration began from the Punjab and also separately, by the early twentieth century, from Gujarat.[26] (When some pioneers settled in Aotearoa they sent news back to their villages for relatives and friends to join them overseas. The latter in turn repeated the process — hence the term 'chain migration'.) Gujaratis and Punjabis had already emigrated to South Africa, Australia, Canada and elsewhere (including Burma, Singapore, Brazil and Argentina), but New Zealand became a sought-after destination once immigration restrictions and discrimination against Indians set in within other white settler colonies during the early twentieth century. Another reason for this southernmost Indian diaspora was because ships with passenger migrants (the name for those who were not indentured migrants) destined for Fiji stopped in Auckland, and some Indians tried to disembark there. Other non-indentured Indians who had originally decided to work in Fiji learned about better opportunities further south.

The sustained waves from the two centres of the Indian diaspora in Punjab and Gujarat to New Zealand were also part of the massive transformations within rural India that pushed global emigration, including to the South Pacific. During the colonial years the cash economy swept through much of Punjab and Gujarat, inducing rural indebtedness, higher taxation, land shortages and environmental degradation, as well as increasing the commercialisation of agriculture and customary services. Cultural pressures, such as expenditure on weddings, houses and other markers of social and religious status, exacerbated the drive for extra income. By the early twentieth century emigration was an accepted practice from

above: Dr Mutyala Satyanand addresses the Auckland Indian Association at a celebration of India's independence, 1947. On his right is Devjibhai Patel and on his left is Mrs Pickett.

below: Jasmine Patel, held by her father, Jagdish Patel, and Kamal Patel, carried by Mrs Patel, with Mr and Mrs Mahendra Thaker, New Zealand's first sponsored Asian refugees from Uganda, at Wellington Airport.

villages in Punjab and South Gujarat — and New Zealand was part of this diaspora.

By 1920, with changes to immigration laws, the curtain fell, excluding almost all Indian immigration to Aotearoa, except where family relationships with Kiwi-Indians already existed. This meant that most Kiwi-Indians until the 1980s originated from Punjab or Gujarat. Immigration exceptions were granted to Anglo-Indians and to a few Indian students and professionals — such as Dr Mutyala Satyanand and Tara Satyanand, who arrived from Fiji during the 1940s — and later to guest workers from Fiji. From 1972 through to 1973, 244 refugees of Indian heritage from Uganda (out of 60,000 expelled from Uganda under President Idi Amin's regime) were relocated to New Zealand, although even this small number attracted controversy and opposition.[27]

The demographic patterns of Kiwi-Indians radically shifted during the late 1980s with new waves of Indian immigration from Fiji, India and other countries. The 1987 Immigration Act opened the way to immigrants with required skills, qualifications or capital to invest, rather than cultural background and nationality. With race no longer grounds for exclusion, new flows of migrants increased from the wider Indian subcontinent. Many new settlers were professionals or business investors. Since the 1980s Indians also came to New Zealand as guest workers, working on market gardens and orchards in Pukekohe, Ohakune, Hawke's Bay, Hamilton and Nelson.

The composition of the local Indian population changed when thousands of Fijians of Indian heritage migrated to New Zealand to escape the civil unrest, economic hardship and discrimination that followed the South Pacific's first military coup d'état in Fiji in May 1987, and the subsequent coups in 2000 and 2006.[28] Indo-Fijians were directly targeted, especially after 1987 and 2000, and thousands fled to New Zealand, Australia, Canada and the United States.[29] Before 1987, some Indo-Fijians had studied in New Zealand; a few permanently settling here. Between 1967 and 1987, other Indo-Fijians had been contracted through the Fijian and New Zealand

Phuman Singh Gill: Early Sikh settler

Phuman Singh Gill, along with his brother Bir (Weer) Singh Gill, was one of the first Sikh and Punjabi settlers in Aotearoa, arriving around 1890.[30] He was not the first Punjabi to settle here,[31] but his remarkable life highlights the mixing of diverse cultures in earlier times. An initial encounter in Auckland was, however, traumatic. He was accosted on the street and his turban was unravelled to reveal his hair, which was kept long according to Sikh custom. After this insult Phuman Singh cut his hair short. A Muslim in Auckland taught Phuman Singh how to make and sell confectionery, and he later went into business with another Muslim in Whanganui. In 1897 Phuman Singh married fellow immigrant Margaret Ford, an English nurse.

The couple established a confectionery and ice-cream business, Abraham Singh & Co., Indian Lolly Manufacturers, with Charlie Abraham. Phuman Singh opened another shop called Eureka, a name given to businesses he set up in New Plymouth and Palmerston North. In 1898, in Whanganui, Margaret gave birth to Ranjit Singh and later to Dhuleep, Esive and Madge. In 1928 Madge married another prominent Sikh immigrant, Santa Singh. Weer Singh Gill married a Māori woman and during World War I he briefly worked as a cook at Trentham Military Camp.

Wedding of Phuman Singh Gill and Margaret Ford, 1897.

Aotearoa's Muslim community: Indian origins

Muslims from the Indian subcontinent were working in Aotearoa since lascars sailed here in 1769, but the first Muslim family to call this land home was probably that of Mahomet and Mindia Wuzerah, among the Indian servants that came with Sir John Cracroft Wilson to Lyttelton in the mid-nineteenth century. Abdullah Drury's historical research suggests the Wuzerahs were a 'distinctly Muslim family consistently treated and regarded in a respectful manner'.[32] There are several other reports of Indian Muslims working and living throughout New Zealand during the nineteenth century.

During the early twentieth century, three Gujarati men arrived who would help establish the Muslim community in Aotearoa New Zealand. Ismail Bhikoo, from the village of Manekpore, arrived in Auckland in 1911; Joseph Moses (known also as Esup Musa or Mussa) came to Auckland from Sitpon in 1912; and Mohammad Kara from Adada arrived in Christchurch in 1907. They were later joined by their families, including two early Indian women immigrants to Aotearoa: Mariam Bhikoo and Bai Bibi Musa.

There are records of other Muslims, especially from Punjab, working and settling during these early years in Aotearoa, but Gujarati Muslims were proactive in establishing the formal associations of both Muslims and Indians. When Aotearoa's Islamic community was small, Gujarati Muslims strongly identified with the wider Indian community: Mohammad Kara was one of the founders of the Christchurch Indian Association in 1937, and Ismail Bhikoo's son, Esup, served as president of the Waikato Indian Association from 1949 to 1951.[33] In 1950, Indian Muslims, along with Muslims of other nationalities, established the New Zealand Muslim Association in Auckland; Suliman Bhikoo (son of Ismail Bhikoo) was the first president, and Ismail Ali Moses (Musa) the first secretary. In 1960, Maulana Ahmed Said Musa Patel arrived in New Zealand to become the country's first *mullah*. By 1963 Auckland Muslims had purchased a house in Ponsonby that would become New Zealand's first *masjid* (mosque); Suliman Bhikoo poured the foundations for Al-Masjid Al-Jamie on 30 March 1979 (opposite).

Meanwhile, Indians were pioneers among the Christchurch Muslim community. In 1977 Suliman Ismail Kara (grandson of Mohammad Kara and active in the Christchurch Indian Association) was the first president of the Muslim Association of Canterbury. This association was one of several groups throughout the country that formed the Federation of Islamic Associations of New Zealand (FIANZ) in 1978. By then the ethnic origins of Aotearoa's Muslims were widening, and included many Muslim immigrants of Indian heritage from Fiji. In New Zealand's 2018 census, 57,276 people of highly diverse ethnicities proclaimed their faith as Muslim. But the establishment of Islam in Aotearoa owes much to the quiet and persistent observance and gentle advocacy of the Indian families that settled in Aotearoa during the early twentieth century.[34]

Suliman Bhikoo pours the foundations for the Al-Masjid Al-Jamie, 30 March 1979.

governments to work in New Zealand under various schemes, mainly in agriculture, forestry and halal slaughtering.

During the twenty-first century, another pathway for Indians to migrate to New Zealand has been through education. The lucrative international student market has become New Zealand's fifth-largest export category. Students from India make up the largest grouping within the non-university tertiary sector, many studying in private institutions. In 2015, 28,505 Indian citizens were full-fee-paying students within New Zealand tertiary institutions. Indian students in New Zealand often work in casual employment, especially within the hospitality industry. There have been cases of exploitation both within New Zealand and from unscrupulous immigration agents in India.[35]

Anti-Asian sentiments and actions thrived within the predominantly white settler colonies of Australia, Canada and South Africa, where a conviction of racial superiority underpinned imperial domination.[36] Joseph Chamberlain, the British Secretary of State for the Colonies, declared in 1895, 'I believe that the British race is the greatest of governing races the world has ever seen.'[37] (To be clear, he was referring to white Britons.) As Lala Lajpat Rai, an Indian freedom fighter and early leader of the Indian National Congress, observed when living in exile in the United States, 'Wherever we look around the Pacific and the Indian ocean — New Zealand, Australia, California, Canada, South Africa — we see the English-speaking faces filled with disquiet raising their defensive walls higher and higher.'[38]

By the late nineteenth century Indians faced discrimination of varying degrees within the colonies of South Africa:[39] having to carry a pass in Natal; paying a poll tax in Transvaal; and in other areas facing restrictions such as curfews over hawking, ownership (of property, retail, liquor), voting, and even walking on footpaths. In 1888 a law in Natal classified Indians as an uncivilised race. Most famously in 1893 in Natal, Mohandas Gandhi, then a lawyer, was ejected from a train. So began his experiences that spurred the non-violent fight against injustice and inequality. In 1907 Gandhi termed this movement *satyagraha* ('holding firmly to truth'), in opposition to the Asiatic Registration Act of 1906 (the Black Act) in Transvaal, which made it compulsory for Indians to be fingerprinted and carry registration documents.

With emigration to South Africa either blocked or made difficult by restrictions, the South Pacific became a destination for Indian migrants. Some migrants first ventured to Africa but returned disillusioned to India. Bhana Chhiba, who would eventually operate several successful fruit and vegetable shops in New Zealand, initially tried to sell produce in Johannesburg during 1906–7, but found the costs of hawkers' licences, and the risk of imprisonment for not paying them, too severe. He returned to Gujarat before sailing to New Zealand in 1913. Other prospective Indian emigrants, such as Jelal Natali and Dayal Wallabh, had permits for South Africa, but changed their minds about migrating there after they learned more about the discrimination Indians faced. They were also deterred by the advent of World War I. During the subsequent decades, Indian residence and movement in South Africa became severely curtailed under apartheid legislation, such as the Group Areas Act 1950, which partitioned racial groups into different urban zones.

In 1976, historian Robert Huttenback wrote that 'Australia was as determined as South Africa to arrest the coloured cancer that lack of vigilance had permitted to grow upon the continent'.[40] This condemnation came only a few years after Australia legally ended the rigid White Australia policy. The 1901 Immigration Restriction Act had imposed a stringent dictation test in any European language that effectively banned almost all Indian immigration to Australia for over 50 years,[41] a barrier that led to many Indians moving to New Zealand. For example, Pal Singh Rijji told Karam Singh that Australia's doors were closed and suggested New Zealand as an

Images in newspapers and magazines in Britain's colonies reflected the attitudes of white settler society towards Indian migrants. G. Ashton's depiction of 'A Hindoo Lodging House' appeared in the *Illustrated Australian News* in 1893.

Sikh passengers aboard the *Komagata Maru* in Vancouver, 1914.

alternative destination. In 1920, Karam Singh and a fellow villager, Milki Ram Fermah, sailed to New Zealand.[42]

Australia's severe immigration restrictions also affected Indians transiting between India and New Zealand. Shipping companies became reluctant to provide passage to Indians because of the penalties levied for passengers who might abscond. Although Harnam Singh had been a resident of Australia and of Spring Creek, Blenheim, in New Zealand for over 25 years and was married to an English woman, he was refused passage through Australia. Instead, he had to travel the circuitous route to India via Argentina and London.[43]

Indians were also excluded from Canada during the early twentieth century. The Immigration Act of 1910 required Indians to pay a $200 bond to land there. Further restrictions were introduced in 1913 with an order-in-council that prohibited the landing at any port in British Columbia of any Indian immigrant who was an artisan, skilled or unskilled worker. In 1914, another order-in-council prohibited the landing of any immigrant who had not made a continuous journey from the country of emigration on a single boat with a through ticket. Since there was no direct steamship service from India, Indians were excluded from Canada. In 1914, when a group of Indians on the ship *Komagata Maru* attempted to emigrate to Canada, most had to return to Calcutta (Kolkata), where the venture ended in tragedy: when a crowd resisted the arrest of the leaders, police opened fire and 20 Sikhs were killed.[44]

Although the United States had a reputation for open immigration, most Indians were excluded through the Naturalization Act of 1906 and the Immigration Act of 1917, the latter excluding people who came from the 'barred zone' of the Asia-Pacific.[45]

Clearly there were huge discrepancies between Indians' status as British subjects and their treatment within the white dominions. In 1922, politician, Indian independence activist and international statesman, V. S. Srinivasa Sastri, on behalf of the government of India, toured Australia, Canada and New Zealand to investigate the conditions of Indians in the white dominions. This followed a resolution from the 1921 Imperial Prime Ministers' Conference 'that there is an incongruity between the position of Indians as an equal member of the British Empire and the existence of disabilities upon British Indians lawfully domiciled in some parts of the Empire'.[46]

Sir Keith Sinclair, who wrote a foundational history of New Zealand in 1959, famously posed the question as to why race relations in New Zealand were better than in South Africa, South Australia or South Dakota.[47] Any such validation to the popular hypothesis of New Zealand's superior record of race relations was radically overturned within later national histories.[48] Erik Olssen, for instance, recently labelled Prime Minister Richard Seddon and his supporters as 'open racists' towards Indians — and Chinese and Syrians — whom they saw as posing a moral and genetic threat to the purity of New Zealand British stock.[49] While most historians' revisionism focused on Māori–Pākehā relations — saying little about the exclusion of other minorities, let alone Indians — differing assessments of a white New Zealand can shed light on the blemishes in New Zealand's history of race relations and treatment of Indians.

As noted, the appropriation of indigenous land and resources was part of the wider imperial project. Nigel Murphy has shown how nation-building and national identity in Aotearoa New Zealand rested upon both the dispossession of Māori and incorporation of Māori (especially through the Treaty, and by conferring an Aryan identity on Māori).[50] He explores how the flip side to nation-building and national identity was imposing borders, notably against the 'Asiatic hordes' or 'Yellow Peril', which by the turn of the twentieth century also included Indians. 'Concepts of whiteness and empire were therefore used to bind a disparate community and create

INDIANS IN NEW ZEALAND

(To the Editor.)

Sir,—The recent discussion in the "Evening Post" arising out of the desire for cheap fruit brought out the fact that some Indians pay over £50 per quarter to sell fruit at bleak street corners. Some years ago the City Fathers decided that the best corner be reserved for an European at £13 17s 6d. Yet the Indians tender over £50 for some less favourable positions. The question arises, is the council exploiting the Indians through their necessity? No one seems to hear of Tory, Liberal, or Labour members of the council protesting. This matter was brought up before the committee of Indians which met the Right Hon. Srinivasa Sastri, who, when he heard the particulars, quietly remarked that it was wicked.

Now let us for contrast glance at the position of Britons in India. All the highest paid official positions are reserved for Europeans; only a few of even the lower commissioned ranks in the Indian Army are occupied by Indians—except in the Indian States. No Indians are admitted into the artillery, engineers, or Aviation Corps, but they are all paid out of Indian revenue.

Recently Major Graham Pole, in the House of Commons, asked the Secretary of State for India two questions, which brought in reply the following figures:—4363 military, Indian medical, and Royal Indian Marine pensioners received £2,083,-958 for the year ending March, 1929. During the same period 3106 pensioners of the Indian Civil Service, Judges of the High Courts, pilot and other services, including the Christian Bishop of Madras, received £1,617,719. All this money, or very nearly all, is spent outside of India, and this is only a portion of the economic drain that India has suffered for over a century.

Letter from the NZ and India League defending Indians working in New Zealand.

a national identity for New Zealand, and this identity was to be White, British and imperial.'[51] Murphy also notes that '[t]he fear of pollution, both moral and racial, and the decline of both the white race and the British Empire, lead to rampant imperialist jingoism and a heightened sense of race consciousness . . . Racial superiority, imperialism, purity and race fitness became central elements in New Zealand's identity.' While I agree with Murphy, it should also be emphasised that economic insecurity bolstered discriminatory discourse and actions.[52]

Scholars of white racism outside New Zealand have located anti-Asian discourse and practices within transnational and post-colonial responses within white-settler colonies as 'part of a common strategy for maintaining white supremacy in the aftermath of empire'.[53] Or as Murphy puts it, skin colour created a bond between the new white settler societies during the late nineteenth century: 'a bond of whiteness and Britishness that overcame national boundaries'.[54] More recent assessments of the history of racism in Aotearoa prioritise 'whiteness',[55] but already by the turn of the last century African-American academic and civil rights activist W. E. B. Du Bois heralded the rising ideology of whiteness and predicted that 'the problem of the twentieth century is the problem of the color-line.'[56] A prediction still applicable to the next century. Du Bois was writing about blatant and violent racial discrimination within the United States; Murphy points out that expressions of whiteness varied between white settler societies, with New Zealand moderating its expression of whiteness to accommodate utopian ideals, but equally upholding and perpetuating white superiority.[57]

The exclusion of Indians, whether physical, institutional, casual or discursive, has been very much part of Aotearoa New Zealand's invisible history. We may call it 'exclusion', and yet, as will become clear, it easily slipped into racism. Race and racism is especially manifested through colour — but, as this book reveals with Indians in Aotearoa, racism extends much further than appearance, touching on issues of nationality, ethnicity, culture, gender, sexuality, class and religion.[58]

Invisible is designed to be read as both a narrative of exclusionary practices against Kiwi-Indians and as a collection of selected documents of that history.

The chapters present a history of inequality and racism that ranges from overt actions and hurtful discourse against Kiwi-Indians to systemic and institutionalised racism, along with the microaggressions that are so often normalised in everyday life.[59]

It would be a gloomy and dark book to only record xenophobia, racism and hatred. Indians have survived and forged communities and been part of wider society, as shown in some of the short narratives presented here.[60] We could call and analyse this as agency, resistance, resilience, pushing back; but I prefer to simply locate texts from Kiwi-Indians within the history of Aotearoa New Zealand. This book suggests that we continually ask, 'Are we one?' and 'What are we — not just as a nation, but more specifically as a humane and inclusive nation?'

two.

Immigration, the Backbone of Aotearoa New Zealand

Immigration restrictions have been the most persistent form of institutional discrimination towards Indians in Aotearoa New Zealand.[1] This was never as severe as that inflicted on the Chinese, who, as noted earlier, were required to pay a poll tax from 1881 until 1944 and faced other immigration barriers. Throughout much of the twentieth century, many New Zealanders have smugly held up the nation's immigration policy as less racist than that of Australia, which had overtly introduced a White Australia policy in 1901. But if we delve into New Zealand's immigration history we find that Indians were discriminated against.

The turning point came in 1920 with the passing of the Immigration Restriction Amendment Act, which required immigrants to apply for a permanent residence permit before arrival. This restricted most new Indian migrants, unless links could be made to existing settlers in the country at the time. Behind the legislation was a white New Zealand immigration policy that operated through guidelines determined and applied by a racially driven bureaucracy. Indeed, historian James Belich has gone so far as to call the New Zealand 'immigration gates an "Aryan New Zealand" policy. The gates tell us not only what the gatekeepers wanted to keep outside but also what they thought, or wanted to think, that they had inside: "98.5 per cent British."'[2]

Ravjibhai Hira: Stopped in Australia, on to Aotearoa

Ravjibhai Hira left his family's farm in Kardipore in Gujarat in 1914 to seek work in Australia.[3] The ship he departed on docked at Sydney, where he not only faced the immigration test, but also was informed that a £100 bond was required before he could disembark. Instead, Ravjibhai remained on the ship until it landed at Auckland, where he cleared immigration despite speaking very little English. For two years he hawked fruit from a basket before taking up the more lucrative but strenuous work of scrub-cutting and milking cows. After World War I, he moved to Wellington and briefly collected bottles before once again hawking fruit. This was casual work, and Ravjibhai later found more secure employment at Murphy's brickyard in Hutt Valley. He returned to fruit and vegetable retailing, eventually purchasing his own shop, which he and his son later expanded into a dairy. The profits from this working life were never high, but through this labour Ravjibhai could support his wife and family in India and enable his son's family to settle in New Zealand. Ravjibhai was a founder of the Wellington Indian Association and the New Zealand Indian Central Association (NZICA), and served as president of the former and vice-president of the latter.

Many Indian men travelled regularly to India to visit family. Gathered here at the Wellington overseas terminal are (from left): Manilal Bhana, Jerambhai Govind, Maganbhai Hira, Vallabhbhai Hira, Bhanabhai Keshav, Ravjibhai Hira, Sukhabhai Dahya Gopal. Behind: Bhulabhai Bhana.

Indians did not face immigration restrictions in New Zealand until the 1899 Immigration Restriction Act, but were targeted as part of the late nineteenth-century clamour to exclude Asians from New Zealand. Prime Minister Richard Seddon gave voice to populism through introducing a succession of bills to restrict Asians from New Zealand. Indians (or Hindoos, as they were called) were lumped in with 'undesirables and Asiatics'. On 4 October 1894 the *New Zealand Times* asked,

> Who are the undesirable? They are the pauper, the criminal, the incurable who is also contagious, the Asiatic whose ways are not as our ways, the contract workman who comes in the shadow of the sweater to crush the life out of the industry of the country — these are the mass which we all call undesirable.

The label 'Assyrian' was also synonymous with non-Chinese Asians. When Minister of Labour William Pember Reeves spoke on the Asiatic and other Immigration Restriction Bill in 1895, he advocated that the 'Assyrian hawker is about as undesirable a person as John Chinaman himself' and pointed out that the Assyrians were Hindoos. 'They do not even produce wealth from the earth as the Chinese do . . . they do not lead sanitary lives. They are not a moral people. They are not a highly civilised people, and in no sense are they a desirable people.' During the 1896 Asiatic Restriction Bill debates, Member of Parliament William Earnshaw advocated that if Seddon aimed to exclude Chinese, 'he should also exclude the greater curse in the country — the Assyrian hawkers'.

The legislative council passed the 1896 Asiatic Restriction Act, but it did not become law because some members protested to the imperial government. Britain did not want to offend non-imperial

Asian countries such as Japan. Instead, the 1899 Immigration Restriction Act satisfied imperial concerns about the free mobility of colonial subjects while attempting to cater to popular demands to bar Asians, including Indians, from New Zealand.

New Zealand followed the 1897 Natal Immigration Act in imposing a quasi-educational test on prospective immigrants to prohibit any person not of British or Irish birth and parentage who failed to complete a language reading test. Intending immigrants had to complete an application in English by filling in the blank spaces; if they had prepared, it was not difficult to pass.

The voyage out was an opportunity to exchange information about life in New Zealand, including advice on meeting entry requirements. Makan Lala was 19 when he sailed to New Zealand with his younger brother. Apparently 'it became known to all voyagers that if they could sign their name in English they could disembark in New Zealand; hence during the rest of the trip they practised their signature in English'.[4] Some migrants simply marked a cross by their name or had a friend sign their forms. Jelal Natali, who had been educated in English, assisted some of his companions, while the young Khusal Madhu guided the hand of an elderly man to sign his form in 1921. Milkhi Ram Fermah and some friends wrote from Bundala to the 'Immigration Department' in Wellington stating that they could speak English and would like to enter New Zealand. Each received a form, which had to be completed and submitted to the district commissioner's office in Jalandhar when applying for a passport. They still had to complete a form in English upon arrival in Auckland in 1920.[5] After Karam Singh Basi wrote a letter in 1920 to New Zealand authorities inquiring about immigration formalities, he was told in reply that if he himself had written the letter, he 'can come to New Zealand any time'.[6] But further leniency towards the entry of Indians into New Zealand did not last.

The 1908 Immigration Restriction Act consolidated existing legislation relating to the educational test and to immigration. An amendment in 1910 aimed to tighten loopholes in the entry

1915/40

C. Form No. 297.]

Certificate of Registration under the Immigration Restriction Amendment Act, 1908.

This is to certify that Govind Ranchhoa. an Indian ~~a Chinese~~ residing in New Zealand, being desirous of leaving New Zealand, has registered his name with me.

If he returns to New Zealand within four years from the date hereof, he will not be liable to submit to the reading-test imposed upon Chinese by section 42 of the Immigration Restriction Act, 1908, if he satisfies a Collector of Customs as to his identity. On return to New Zealand the tax will be received on deposit, and will be returned upon identification.

Collector of Customs.

Port of Auckland

Dated 22 July, 1915

Signature of Govind Ranchhoa.

~~In Chinese characters:~~

In English (if possible):

Govind Ranchhod

The thumb-prints of Govind Ranchhoa. attached hereto, were recorded in my presence.

, Collector.

STATEMENT of personal appearance, such as height, build, and other particulars aiding identification

Scar on right temple

LEFT HAND. Plain Impression of Thumb.	RIGHT HAND. Plain Impression of Thumb.

500/4/15—53351

Govind Ranchhod, certificate of registration, 1915.

procedures. Customs officers could choose from four different forms to present to the intending immigrant.

A 1914 draft of the Immigration Restriction Amendment Bill set out to further restrict Indians; where once they simply filled out a form, they would now have to take a dictation test that involved 'copying, in not more than twenty minutes, fifty words in any European language dictated by a Customs officer or an interpreter'. The New Zealand government's stated aim was to

> keep the country clear of coloured and undesirable immigrants, and has provided safeguards against the admission of illiterate Hindus who were threatening to flood the country . . . The amending Bill eliminates the term 'British subjects' from the principal Act, thus doing away with the possibility of the illiterate Hindu being regarded as a British subject in law.[7]

War broke out in August 1914, and India's cooperation was essential, so the bill was dropped.

Before 1920, Indian migrants became resourceful at finding ways to pass the education tests administered by customs officers upon arrival in New Zealand. Some attended 'cramming schools' in Fiji, where they were coached by enterprising 'teachers' to memorise the immigration application forms and prospective answers to questions that might be given by customs officers. Preparation for immigration to New Zealand in Fiji could be at a cost: apparently one teacher, a Parsi, charged a bond of £100 for facilitating immigration to New Zealand, and if this was successful, he received £10 commission.[8] Joala Singh Belling sailed to Fiji to join one of these schools after he failed the education test when he tried to disembark in Auckland. When he returned to New Zealand in 1917 he passed the test.[9]

Indians being transferred from an island steamer to RMS *Niagara* at Auckland, after failing to pass the education test, July 1914.

'A Horde of Hindu Hawkers'

The *NZ Truth* published these alarmist headlines from New Year's Day in 1912, when 80 Punjabis arrived on the *Aparima*, which docked at Auckland en route from Calcutta to Fiji. Only 10 of these passengers intended to stay in Auckland, and several failed the education test or were declared medically unfit. This did not stop *Truth* from despairing that 'a White New Zealand is impossible! The administration of the Alien Immigration or Restriction Act has certainly been effective in one o[r] two respects. In other respects it has been farcical . . . [and it] is no idle thought that some day Australasia will be invaded by hordes of colored men. Where then will the mere handful of whites be? If we are lax today in admitting colored men to our country, if we are unable to resist a peaceable occupation of 80 Hindus, where shall we be when it is as many millions?'[10]

A WHITE NEW ZEALAND.

A HORDE OF HINDU HAWKERS.

An Ineffective Barrier,

LESSONS WHICH SHOULD BE LEARNED.

Alarmist headlines from *NZ Truth*, 1912.

White racism and the push for immigration exclusion directed at Indians peaked after World War I. The Returned Soldiers' Association led the battle-cry; xenophobia flourished among men severely hit by postwar unemployment. Returned servicemen believed they had a right to farm land and that they should not have to compete with foreigners. Government economic policy was largely ineffective at remedying the postwar economic slump, but it did respond to populist demands for immigration controls.

On 11 August 1920, Prime Minister William Massey introduced a bill to amend the Immigration Restriction Act.[11] Three months later, the bill was law,[12] but it had a much longer gestation. 'The Act,' writes Nigel Murphy, 'gave Government complete control over who was able to enter the country and was therefore the culmination of 40 years of legislation and the solution to making a White New Zealand.'[13] Massey himself said as much: 'The Bill is the result of a deep-seated sentiment on the part of a large majority of the people in this country that this Dominion shall be what is often called a "white" New Zealand, and that people who come here should, as far as it is possible for us to provide for it, be of the same way of thinking from the British Empire's point of view.'[14]

The bill also reflected discourse that Indians in New Zealand created as large a problem as the Chinese. The member for Waitematā, Alexander Harris, hoped the bill would 'be found sufficient to control, if not totally exclude, the Indian influx also'.[15]

The 1920 Immigration Restriction Amendment Act replaced the education test with an individual permit system under the authority of the minister of customs. No discussion or appeals were allowed over his decision. The act stipulated:

> (1) No person other than a person of British birth and parentage shall (except as by this Act is specially provided) enter into New Zealand unless he is in possession of a permit to enter in the form and to the effect provided by regulations under this Act.
>
> (2) A person shall not be deemed to be of British birth and parentage by reason that he or his parents or either of them is a naturalised British subject, or by reason that he is an aboriginal native or the descendant of an aboriginal native of any dominion other than the Dominion of New Zealand or of any colony or other possession or of any protectorate of His Majesty.[16]

Khamais 'Jim' Khan: What the records tell us

Khamais 'Jim' Khan made several trips between the Waikato and his home village of Atta, near Jalandhar in Punjab. Born in 1891, he worked in Fiji before arriving in New Zealand in 1918. He was issued with alien re-entry certificates in 1918, 1921 and 1925 for travel to India, probably via Australia. Historian Abdullah Drury has researched Khamais' history through the surviving records.[17]

In 1928 Khamais Khan lived on Cadman Road in Paeroa, in eastern Waikato, while working at a flax mill. In 1935 he worked for the Alderson brothers in Te Papa, within the Aria valley, digging drains. On the 1946, 1949, 1954 and 1969 electoral rolls his residence remained in Aria.

He had retired by 1969, and the 1972 electoral roll shows that he was by then a pensioner in the hospital at Te Kuiti. Burial records reveal that Khamais was buried in Aria on 28 July 1972 with apparently no family or descendants in New Zealand.

opposite: Khamias Khan's certificate of registration, issued in 1918, allowed him to travel to India and return to New Zealand without having to submit to the education test that new migrants had to pass to be allowed to enter the country.

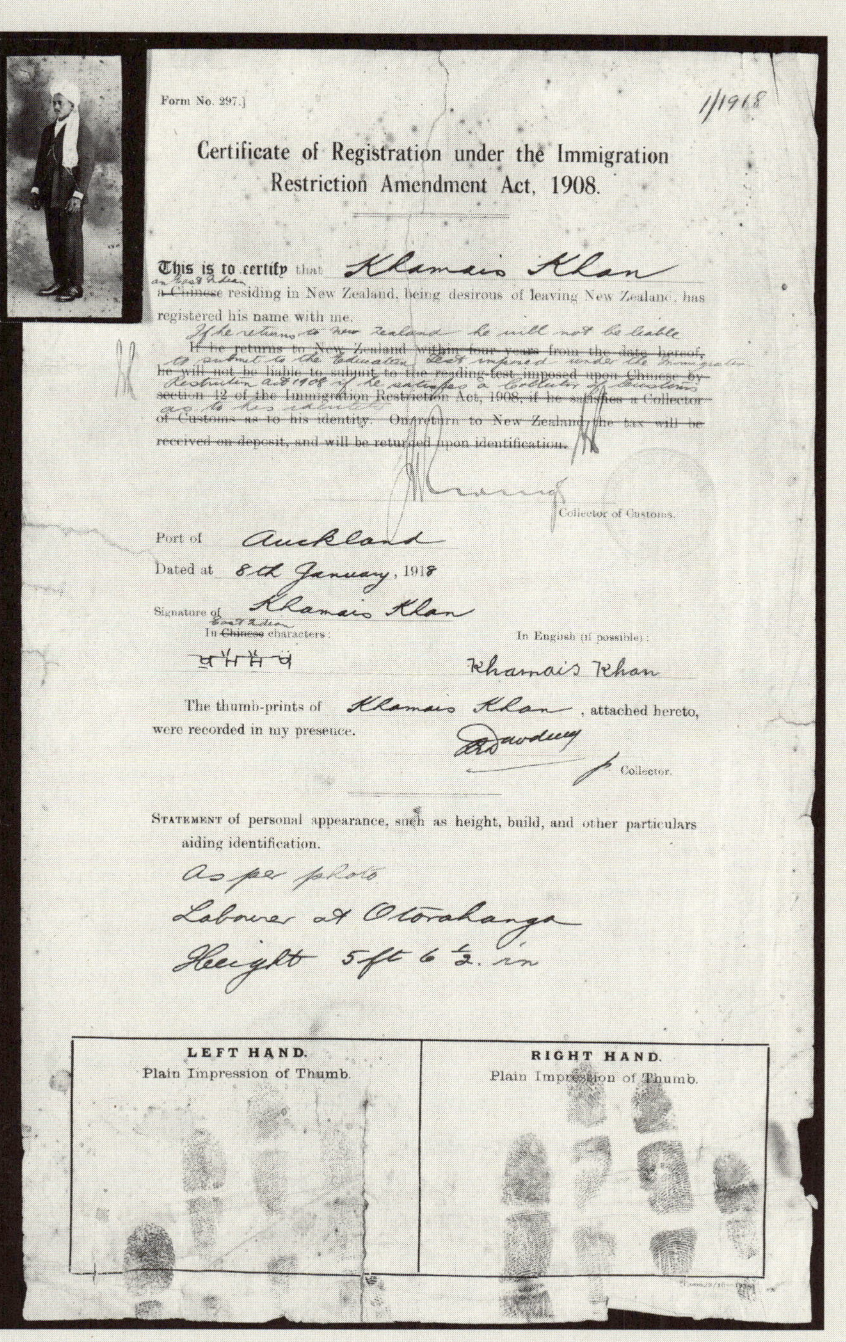

Form No. 297.] 1/1918

Certificate of Registration under the Immigration Restriction Amendment Act, 1908.

This is to certify that Khamais Khan ~~a Chinese~~ An East Indian residing in New Zealand, being desirous of leaving New Zealand, has registered his name with me.

If he returns to New Zealand he will not be liable to submit to the Education Test imposed under the Immigration Restriction Act 1908 if he satisfies a Collector of Customs as to his identity.

~~If he returns to New Zealand within four years from the date hereof, he will not be liable to submit to the reading-test imposed upon Chinese by section 12 of the Immigration Restriction Act, 1908, if he satisfies a Collector of Customs as to his identity. On return to New Zealand the tax will be received on deposit, and will be returned upon identification.~~

Collector of Customs.

Port of Auckland

Dated at 8th January, 1918

Signature of Khamais Khan

In ~~Chinese~~ East Indian characters: [illegible]

In English (if possible): Khamais Khan

The thumb-prints of Khamais Khan, attached hereto, were recorded in my presence.

Collector.

Statement of personal appearance, such as height, build, and other particulars aiding identification.

As per photo
Labourer at Otorohanga
Height 5 ft 6½ in

LEFT HAND. Plain Impression of Thumb.	RIGHT HAND. Plain Impression of Thumb.

Salaam, Sahib! Salaam!
'FILTH IN FIJI. HINDU COOLIE AND HIS CUSTOMS'

These were the racist headlines written by 'Te Pana' in the Returned Soldiers' Association (RSA) publication *Quick March* in 1920. Fiji was described as 'a jumping-off place for Indians with eyes and minds and hearts set on the business channels in New Zealand', where they attended 'cram schools'.

'[Candidates,] . . . with clean starched collars and new suits, drift along the muddy tracks carefully picking their way. They are happy and chatter away in mongrel Hindustani. Three of the number are chanting various sentences in English, repeating over and over again the same words. Tomorrow they leave for New Zealand. They are memorising the necessary 'test' therewith to greet the Customs official at Auckland. If you listen you may hear the same English sounds coming from twenty filthy hovels on the roadside.'[18]

Indians now had to acquire an entry permit, as they were not of British birth and parentage, even though they were British subjects. Application for the permit had to be made before departure from India. Indians who arrived in New Zealand without one were deemed to be prohibited immigrants and refused permission to land, although Europeans who were not British were issued with permits upon arrival.[19] Applications for entry were decided on an individual basis, but in fact provisions allowed for government to exempt specified nations or peoples.

The 1917 and 1918 Imperial War Conferences had established a framework that enabled the dominions to introduce legislation to control Indian immigration. This was through the principle of reciprocity of treatment between India and the self-governing

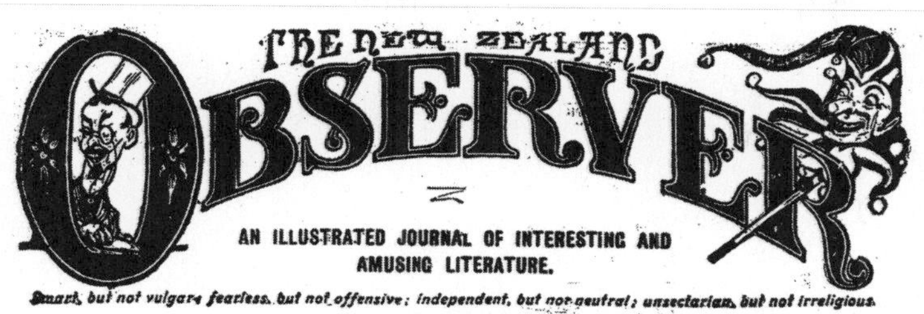

THE NEW ZEALAND

OBSERVER

AN ILLUSTRATED JOURNAL OF INTERESTING AND AMUSING LITERATURE.

Smart, but not vulgar; fearless, but not offensive; independent, but not neutral; unsectarian, but not irreligious.

ESTABLISHED 1880.

VOL. XL.—No. 45.] SATURDAY, JULY 10, 1920. [SIXPENCE.

THE PERIL.

New Zealand Observer, 10 July 1920

Fears over the influx of Asians did not reflect the numbers. At the 1921 census there were only 671 Indians living in Aotearoa.

THE ASIATIC INFLUX.

PROTEST BY SOLDIERS.

INDIGNATION EXPRESSED.

REMIT FOR CONFERENCE.

Protests against the continued influx into New Zealand of Asiatics were voiced at last evening's meeting of the Auckland Returned Soldiers' Association. The matter came up when the following remit to the forthcoming conference in Wellington was put forward for adoption :—

"That the attention of the Government be drawn to the large influx of Hindus and Chinese to the Dominion, and that it be requested to introduce legislation during the coming session to restrict such immigration; and that each association throughout New Zealand be requested to convene a public meeting in its district prior to the meeting of Parliament, to protest against the unrestricted influx of Hindus and Chinese."

New Zealand Herald, 26 May 1920

After 1918 anti-immigration sentiment in New Zealand ran high, and there was anger over the perceived unrestricted entry of Indian and Chinese migrants.

"THE THIN RED LINE OF KINSHIP THROUGH OUR VEINS RUNS WARM."

New Zealand Observer, 29 May 1920

dominions. British citizens domiciled in any country of the empire, including India, were to be admitted into any other country of the empire for visits, and for the purposes of pleasure, commerce or education. Indian men, already permanently resident in imperial countries, could bring in their wives and children aged under 21 years.

The New Zealand government announced in June 1921 that Indians could emigrate to New Zealand if they were 'the wives and minor children of permanent residents of New Zealand'. By 1925, Indian male residents in New Zealand had to produce an official certificate verifying their status before permits were issued for their wife and children. A statutory declaration in English, signed before a Justice of the Peace in New Zealand, was also required. The provision for Indian men to have their immediate family join them was particularly significant for the future shape of the Kiwi-Indian community. New adult male Indian immigration was severely restricted after 1920, as noted above, but immediate family reunification was permitted. The 1920 Immigration Restriction Amendment Act remained the basis of Indian immigration to Aotearoa New Zealand until 1987. Some Indians found other ways to emigrate there, illegally or legally, such as on a temporary student permit. Once qualified and employed in a profession, they could seek permanent residence.

Despite their small numbers (671 at the 1921 census), there were protests from Indians living in Aotearoa over the 1920 Immigration Restriction Amendment Act. Chhotu Jivanji, representing the Auckland Indian Association, wrote to Prime Minister William Massey objecting to the inclusion of Indians in the act.[20] Chhotubhai sent a copy of his letter to the Indian Overseas Association, who

Vol. XXI.—No. 1067. WEDNESDAY, DECEMBER 1, 1920. Sixpence.

THE ALIEN WAVE.

Sir William Herries remarked one day last week that there was nothing in the existing legislation to prevent the present drift of alien immigration to New Zealand.

New Zealand: "Gee! How do they expect me to keep out that lot with a broom like this!"

Free Lance, 1 December 1920

Concerns flourished over the inability of legislation to control Asian immigration.

raised the legislation with the Secretary of State for India. This protest drew attention to the plight of 140 Indians who were caught by the sudden change to New Zealand's immigration legislation. They had sailed for New Zealand via Fiji before the new law was passed but, due to shipping difficulties and strikes in Fiji, they were delayed for up to six months. Not only had this delay forced many to find work in Suva, but also their expenses soared when shipping companies increased the bonds for passages from £100 to £150 after the 1920 act came into force. The bond was imposed because shipping companies were held responsible for any costs in deportation and the recovery of absconding illegal immigrants. The New Zealand government finally allowed those who had left India before 21 November 1920 to land under the old immigration provisions.[21]

The majority of adult Indian males who migrated to New Zealand before World War II had wives and children in India. Periodic visits back home were usually made to families, when migrants might build a new house, attend to farming and business matters, oversee family milestones such as weddings, and participate in village and political affairs. These visits sustained intimacy between partners who had been estranged for long periods, so this could be a time when another child might be conceived. Visits to India could not be rushed. They were also expensive; there was not just the cost of the journey, but a migrant would not return to their village empty-handed. Travel times and distances were lengthy and often unpredictable, especially when undertaken by sea.

Indians who left New Zealand after 1920 required a re-entry permit or certificate of registration if they were to return.[22] These permits were issued to Indians for four years, but frequently this

Bhanu Daji: Through a child's eyes

When Bhanu Daji was a child she made the journey from Karadi in Gujarat to New Zealand in 1953, with her sisters Laxmi and Damyanti and her mother, Gangaben Ravji.[23] The family was migrating to be with their father and Gangaben's husband, Jerambhai Ravji, who had joined his father in Aotearoa in 1928. Jerambhai returned periodically to Karadi and during World War II he and Gangaben were active in civil disobedience against British rule.[24] The couple had been betrothed to each at about the age of six.

Bhanu recalls the voyage on the *Strathmore*: '[W]e were confronted with many new and different things: seeing white people for the first time (there were no white people living in the vicinity of our villages), hearing them speak in another language and a different way of dressing. The food and drinks were also foreign to us so whenever we approached the dining area for meals the smell of cooked food would make us want to throw up. We immediately escaped to the sanctuary of our cabins where we would dine on teekhi (spiced) puris and chivda (mixed bhuja) which Mum had made back home and brought on the ship. We also stockpiled the cabin crackers, which were left with room service each day, to keep the hunger pangs at bay – it was good to eat something new for a change!

'Another barrier we faced was the English language. Some of the Indian families on board were making a return trip to New Zealand and so were already fluent in English. They were able to guide us on how to use the toilets and the bathrooms . . . our father had made sure we wouldn't travel alone and we were accompanied by friends who looked after us on our journey. The children we played with gave us chewing gum, telling us it was lollies, and would laugh at us when we swallowed it.'

Bhanu Daji (nearest to car) with her mother, Ganga Ravji, and family, circa late 1950s.

In 2019, Bhanu's parents became New Zealand's — possibly the world's — longest-married living couple, after 84 years together.[25]

Although many families from India were happily reunited after World War II, older children, especially those aged over 21 years, remained in India. According to Ajit Singh, the 'left behind' often endured trauma, hardship, loneliness and mental stress.[26]

Young jahaji: A long and daunting voyage

After the 1920 Immigration Restriction Amendment Act, several young Indian males joined their fathers, grandfathers and other kin in Aotearoa. The children often sailed together in groups, under the care of a parent or village friend, and were called *jahaji* (*jahazi* in Punjabi) as they were fellow passengers or 'mates'. Ganesh Sukha, one jahaji, formed long-term friendships with a group of five boys when he emigrated to New Zealand in 1923. They slept in bunks and cooked their own meals. For many the long voyage out was when they were suddenly thrown into new gender roles – cooking and washing their clothes and dishes – typically women's work in the village. These new tasks helped to relieve the monotony of the voyage and prepared the young men for living in mostly male households as migrants.

In 1911, Nand Singh Bukkan, aged 17, and four friends, Nand Singh, Gajan Singh, Geena Singh and Briam Singh, left their village of Sultanpur in Punjab to sail from Calcutta to Fiji. They travelled for six months, probably via Singapore and Australia; 'a very long and exhausting journey combined with bad weather at sea'.[27] In 1913 Bukkan and his friends left Fiji for New Zealand where they had heard that work was available.

It could be daunting for young Gujarati vegetarians to prepare and eat new food, especially the meat products available on the steamers, although ships chartered for Indians may have provided pulses and rice. Some children tried to periodically fast or subsist off sweets, bread, tea, pickles or other food that had been provided from home. Ganesh's passage cost half that which Bawa Kana paid for his sons to travel from Mumbai to Wellington: Hira, aged 16 in 1924, who sailed in the care of 10 *jahaji*; Jivan, aged 11 in 1927; and Lala, aged 13 in 1928.[28] The more expensive passages provided beds and substantial meals. As Hirabhai recalled, for young *jahaji* the voyage was one of excitement mingled with loneliness and bewilderment; it was also an opportunity to exchange information about life in New Zealand, including advice on how to deal with immigration formalities.

period was too short and could be extended for up to 10 years. Many Indians who had returned to India before World War II were delayed from returning because of the shortage of shipping available for civilians after the war. Their re-entry permits expired and they or their sons were prohibited from entering New Zealand. Some of these sons would have been able to join their fathers in New Zealand under the 1920 Immigration Act if they were under 21 years, but the sons were too old after the war, while some who were within the qualifying age were denied entry because their fathers had died.

A deputation from the New Zealand Indian Central Association met with Walter Nash, the minister of customs, but no exemptions were given to the prohibition. Bob Semple, the minister for lands, presented a petition, on behalf of the NZICA, to government. Although the Public Petitions Committee recommended government allow up to 15 individuals to be admitted to New Zealand, the Customs Department still would not budge.[29] On 12 April 1947, Kana Natha Patel, on behalf of 103 Gujarati passengers destined for New Zealand, wrote to the Commonwealth Relations Department of the government of India about their plight. The case was then taken up by the Indian government, which lobbied for the entry into New Zealand of seven children whose fathers had died. Entry for some of these was eventually granted.[30]

Under the British Nationality and New Zealand Citizenship Act of 1948, all British subjects, including Indians, who were permanently resident in New Zealand that year acquired New Zealand citizenship. There was still, however, some confusion over whether Indians who were permanently resident in New Zealand were required to hold a certificate of registration for re-entry if they left New Zealand and wanted to return.[31] Citizenship

To the Honourable the Speaker and Members of the House of Representatives of the Dominion of New Zealand in Parliament assembled

The Petition of The NEW ZEALAND INDIAN CENTRAL ASSOCIATION INCORPORATED , *of* WELLINGTON.

HUMBLY SHOWETH:—

[Leg.—55. [1,000/10/45—10656

1. *That* your petitioner, The New Zealand Indian Central Association Incorporated, was formed in 1927. It has seven branches:

(a) Auckland Indian Association Inc.

(b) Pukekohe Indian Association.

(c) Rotorua Indian Association.

(d) N.Z. Indian Association - Country Section.

(e) Manawatu - Hawkes Bay Indian Association.

(f) Wellington Indian Association Inc.

(g) Christchurch Indian Association.

It is estimated that there are approximately nine hundred Indians of full blood at present resident in New Zealand and your petitioner with its four hundred and twentytwo members, all of full blood over twentyone years of age, and their wives and children estimated at one hundred andfifty, is, therefore, actively supported by over 60% of the Indians of full blood resident in New Zealand today.

2. That The Indian community in New Zealand, through your petitioner, is most anxious to make submissions to The Honourable the Speaker and Members of the House of Representatives of the Dominion of New Zealand in Parliament assembled regarding the unfortunate position of a number of Indians, otherwise eligible for entry into New Zealand, who, through circumstances solely associated with transport difficulties during the recent war, have been unable to enter New Zealand within the period and under the conditions provided for in entry permits already granted to them.

3. That The conditions under which Indians are allowed and have since prior to the recent war been allowed to enter New Zealand are :

but to present this present petition.

8. That the point which your petitioner desires respectfully to stress is that if it had not been for the outbreak of war and the consequent cessation of transport between India and New Zealand the Indians concerned would be permanently resident in New Zealand today and the fact that they are not so resident does not in any way whatsoever arise from their own default or from any circumstances within their control.

9. That your petitioner will have no difficulty in establishing that the men concerned are of excellent character and if allowed into New Zealand will prove hard working industrious and good citizens. Suitable guarantees can be arranged, if they are requested, that these men can be found employment and that they will not become a charge upon the state.

10. That the address of your petitioner is care of Messieurs J.J. & Denis McGrath, Solicitors, 10 Woodward Street, Wellington.

YOUR PETITIONER THEREFORE HUMBLY PRAYS that your Honourable House will be pleased :-

(a) to make provision for the entry into New Zealand of the Indians in the groups set out above and
or

G.N. H.D. (b) to grant such further/other relief as it thinks fit.

And your petitioner, as in duty bound, will ever pray.

The Seal of the New Zealand)
Indian Central Association)
Incorporated was hereunto)
affixed in the presence of:)

THE N.Z. INDIAN CENTRAL
COMMON SEAL
ASSOCIATION INC.

G. Nages. President.

H. Dahya Secretary.

opposite and above: Part of a petition from the New Zealand Indian Central Association seeking assistance for Indians who had been delayed in sailing to New Zealand because of the shipping difficulties caused by World War II.

was further complicated for Kiwi-Indians who were born in India's princely states, such as several Gujaratis from the state of Baroda. Although those Indians had British Protected status, they were not British citizens. Technically these people were stateless, but provision was made to register as Indian citizens after India's independence in 1947. If they had emigrated to New Zealand before 1948 they were deemed 'aliens' and had to apply for naturalisation before they could be granted New Zealand citizenship.

On 13 March 1951, the New Zealand government limited re-entry permits for Indians to 18 months;[32] a move designed to encourage Kiwi-Indians to bring their wives and children to New Zealand and to force assimilation among Indians before they were 'teens fully indoctrinated in the Asiatic way of life'.[33] The director of employment even proposed an immigration bill to deny Indians from registration as New Zealand citizens if they refused to bring their wives with them. Economics were given as the rationale; remittances and money spent by Kiwi-Indians while in India were seen as a heavy drain on overseas funds.[34]

Note the discriminatory nature of the policy: Indians born in New Zealand could leave for 18 months only if they held a certificate of registration, but recent Anglo-Indian migrants were exempted. Indians in New Zealand, including General K. M. Carriappa, the Indian High Commissioner, protested about the severe restrictions.[35] It was not until 1957 that the minister of immigration reintroduced four-year re-entry permits.[36] Nor is it clear how long the four-year permits remained, or when re-entry permits were abolished. By 1971 NZICA noted that government policy towards Indian citizens in New Zealand 'included the change from the 18-month re-entry period to the present time of the period of the validity of the individual's passport'.[37]

This photograph was taken in Wellington in 1940, when World War II disrupted the usual travel between India and New Zealand, separating families for many years. From left: Mihan Singh, who arrived in Aotearoa in 1913; his son Balwant Singh Nagra, who arrived in 1936; Chanan Singh; an unnamed customs officer; Chanan Singh's father, Genda Singh; and Bujha Ram.

Certificates of registration: Chinese and Indians

'The Government has decided that Certificates of Registration issued to Chinese and Indians permanently resident in New Zealand are in the future to be valid for re-entry into this country for a period of eighteen months from the date of issue only. I should be obliged if you would ensure that any Certificates issued by you after receipt of this memorandum are suitably amended before being handed to the holder. No exceptions to this policy will be made and it is most important that no certificate be issued in error or otherwise, which is not limited in validity to eighteen months. This memorandum should be brought to the notice of all officers handling Certificates of Registration including the Boarding Inspector and his staff at main ports. 'Chinese' are to be regarded as all persons of Chinese extraction whatever their nationality (therefore including Chinese born in New Zealand), and 'Indians' as all persons of Indian race wherever born but not including members of the group of Anglo-Indians who have migrated to New Zealand since the recent war. Chinese and Indians should be warned that extensions of the validity of their Certificates of Registration will not be granted should they make application from overseas, for such extensions.'[38]

— Customs Department memorandum, 9 April 1951

Under the workings of the 1920 Immigration Restriction Amendment Act, Indian women in New Zealand — those born here as well as permanent residents — were prohibited, except under exceptional circumstances, from having their fiancé or husband (whom they had married overseas) join them in New Zealand. Government expected these women to move to India to live with their husband. Yet a bride was able to join her partner in New Zealand.

The Indian community became outraged, especially after World War II as the numbers of Indian women in New Zealand increased. After all, postwar immigration policies insisted Indian mothers accompany children to New Zealand; but if they were to give birth to children here, what marriage prospects did their daughters have? Ganda Nager, NZICA's secretary, protested to the minister of immigration, Ralph Hanan, about this anomaly that discriminated on the basis of ethnicity and gender: '[T]hose that are lucky enough to find young men who are not related have married in New Zealand . . . could it be possible Sir, for you to give consent to the girls to come back to New Zealand with their husbands?'[39]

Staff advised the minister that the Indian community (2435 at the 1951 census) was not too closely related to form marriages in New Zealand, and that '[t]he real background is a desire to import more Hindu workers'. Nager was told by the immigration minister that 'the normal practice is for the wife to join and live with her husband, particularly where two countries are involved. Our general immigration policy is framed accordingly.' By 1960, after continued lobbying from NZICA, the practice of prohibiting intending bridegrooms from living in New Zealand was lifted.[40]

Was Aotearoa New Zealand's immigration permit system discriminatory towards Indians? Media in Ceylon (Sri Lanka) posed the question in 1948 to Prime Minister Peter Fraser: Did New Zealand have its own White Australia policy? He fudged the answer, claiming that there was no discrimination against Indians in New Zealand 'because no white policy on Australian lines operated there'.[41] Practices that enabled discrimination against Indian immigration could be found, however, within confidential government memos:

> Our immigration is based firmly on the principle that we are and intend to remain a country of European development. It is inevitably discriminatory against Asians — indeed against all persons who are not wholly of European race and colour. Whereas we have done much to encourage immigration from Europe, we do everything to discourage it from Asia.[42]

Compare those private words with a public memorandum from the government: 'No statutory provision is at present in force which specifically restricts entry into New Zealand on the basis of race, religion or nationality.'[43] Historian Sean Brawley saw this divergence in New Zealand's Asian immigration policy as blurring fact and fiction. 'The fact is that for much of the postwar period New Zealand maintained a policy which can be most conveniently labelled the "White New Zealand Policy", but sought to hide this fact from the international community through a variety of techniques.'[44] Political scientist Theo Roy reiterated that New Zealand's immigration legislation and practices remained discriminatory during the 1960s, operating a white New Zealand policy despite an outward show of 'domestic inter-racial harmony'.[45]

Kiwi-Indians, along with Chinese and Māori, also continued to face discrimination when visiting or transiting through Australia. They were only granted a 72-hour transit visa, but other New Zealanders did not require a visa or were stamped with an automatic three-month visa upon arrival in Australia. As Nigel Murphy explains, 'Although not a New Zealand policy, the New Zealand government tacitly agreed with the Australian Government, and offered no assistance to Indian and Chinese New Zealanders' campaign to remove it.'[46] NZICA and the New Zealand Chinese Association lobbied the New Zealand and Australian governments, and in 1972 Chinese and Indian New Zealanders were granted equal rights of entry with other New Zealanders.

The 1964 Immigration Act introduced an exemption that enabled any citizen of a Commonwealth country or Ireland, regardless of race, to enter New Zealand without a permit if they had qualified for permanent residency in Australia.[47] Few Indians had by then attained residency in Australia, and so they were prohibited from emigrating to New Zealand. By 1966 some Indian professionals were admitted as permanent residents to New Zealand.

Immigration law changed again during the 1970s under the Labour government of Norman Kirk, who advocated policy that ignored prospective migrants' race, colour and religion.[48] During the 1970s an NZICA immigration committee (President Lalbhai Patel, with Raman Ganda, Dayal Kesry, Harbans Randhawa Singh and Govind Bhula) pushed for immigration policy liberalisation, similar to the Canadian points system.[49] After the immigration policy review of 1974, all prospective emigrants, including those from the United Kingdom, required a permit before leaving for New Zealand, while permanent entry was determined on the basis of New Zealand's demand for skills and qualifications. While this marked an official end to a white immigration policy, unofficially a preference remained for white migrants from northern Europe.

Following the Citizenship Act 1977, immigration criteria widened in 1978, and were further clarified with the 1987 Immigration Act on occupation, family reunification and humanitarian grounds, with more business and professional immigrants being admitted to New Zealand. During the following decades, the number of Indian migrants to Aotearoa subsequently grew, but with this came public alarm about the numbers of Indians here — a clamour redolent of anti-Indian hysteria during the early twentieth century.

Savitaben Babubhai Ghelabhai: Persistence pays off

Savita Babu Ghela may have been the first Indian woman to be allowed by the government to have her husband join her in New Zealand. Savita Ghela (née Morar) was born in Navsari, Gujarat in 1935 and came to New Zealand as a four-year-old in 1939 with her mother, Mani Morar, to join Mani's husband, Lalloo Morar. He had emigrated to Aotearoa in 1920.

Savitaben attended Mount Cook School and Johnsonville Main in Wellington. At the age of 16, Savita went to India with her family to find a suitable marriage proposal.

After her arranged marriage to Babubhai Ghelabhai in 1951, she stayed with her husband in Navsari for seven years, unable to return to New Zealand. Savitaben wrote a heartfelt letter begging the New Zealand authorities to allow her to return with her husband.

Savita's father, Lalloo, who was a naturalised New Zealand citizen and a well-respected member of the Indian community, also wrote to Labour member of Parliament Henry May, along with letters of support from the Wellington Indian Association. Eventually the couple were granted permission to migrate to New Zealand where they would successfully run Ghela's dairy in Johnsonville.

Savitaben died on 13 August 2020, aged 84 years.[50]

Savita Ghela (seated) with (from left) Prime Minister Sir Walter Nash, Babubhai Ghelabhai (husband), Sharda Amrat Dullabh and Amratbhai Dullabh (from the Wellington Indian Association) at the New Zealand Labour Party Debutantes' Ball held at Wellington Town Hall, circa 1958–60.

Savita Ghela (née Morar, second row at left) with her classmates at Johnsonville Main School in 1948, a few years after she arrived in New Zealand with her mother.

three.

White Race Organisations

The history of Kiwi-Indians was at its most uncomfortable in Pukekohe, where the White New Zealand League emerged during the 1920s and discrimination against Indians continued long afterwards. This is where a history of racism is perhaps most disturbing because, unlike racism projected through immigration or work, or sporadic outbursts of verbal and physical violence, the racism at Pukekohe became embedded in the community — where Indians settled, worked, played sport, attended school and participated in local events.

Since around 1912 Indians have had a long and continuous history of settlement at Pukekohe.[1] The township was home also to Māori and Chinese, who were also the targets of racism from the Pākehā majority.[2] Pukekohe's ethnic history is complex, and many present-day members of the community do not want to drag up past racism.[3] In 2003 the Pukekohe Indian Association celebrated the fiftieth anniversary of its headquarters, Nehru Hall. The town's mayor, Heather Maloney, apologised for the 'past injustices' that the Indian community had encountered.[4]

White racism at Pukekohe, while localised and extreme, nonetheless had widespread support throughout the country. Other white racist organisations pre-date the White New Zealand League, and re-emerged long after the league's demise. Much of this chapter focuses on Pukekohe, yet the underbelly of white racism and pro-white organisations could be found within several other communities throughout the nation. Today the internet enables such venom to spread across localised communities. When we untangle New Zealand's history of pro-white organisations, we find that international links and discourse, spread through newspapers, also propelled and nurtured these exclusionary and anti-Asian bodies, decades before the internet was invented.

The names of various anti-Asian organisations in the early twentieth century were self-explanatory: Asiatic Immigration Restriction League, Anti-Asiatic League, White Race League.[5] Although Chinese were the principal focus of these early organisations, Indians were also targeted. In 1907 the Asiatic Immigration Restriction League established branches in several towns in the Wairarapa and in Wellington, urging the restriction — indeed, the prohibition — of further Asian immigration. Its motto was 'A White New Zealand'. The White Race League, founded in Wellington in 1907, demanded that the 'white race should only trade with the white race'.[6] The league's objectives were:

1. The preservation and development of the white race.
2. The discussion, extension, and dissemination of the ideals which should inspire the leading members of the white race.
3. The earnest study of social problems bearing on the welfare of humanity and the dissemination of knowledge concerning such problems.
4. The institution of groups of social volunteers, who

THE COMING ARTIST.

New Zealand Observer, 26 April 1919

Fears that 'white' New Zealand was being threatened by an influx of Asian migrants was reflected in local newspapers.

will undertake the practical work which the higher humanity may demand.

5. The formation of the league in New Zealand, with power to extend its organisation to other countries.[7]

Even the Ku Klux Klan (KKK) found support in New Zealand. After a retired Presbyterian minister, B. Hutson, from New Jersey in the United States, toured New Zealand in 1923, KKK branches were formed in Auckland and Wellington to stop 'Oriental' migration. It claimed to be a 'great secret society opposed to Asiatic labour', with around 1000 members in Auckland. The 'central fact at the back of the formation . . . is antagonism to Asiatic labour. The Chinese and the Indians are mentioned as the two races to which the

University of Auckland capping parade on Karangahape Road, Auckland, 1923.

Klan has most objection.'[8] The Klan aimed to garner support from Freemasons, Foresters, Oddfellows and Orangemen.

The same year, Auckland university students, dressed as klansmen, rode horses in the capping carnival parade along Karangahape Road to advertise the students' carnival play, 'Blu Blux Blan'. Apparently 'other Aucklanders wore the white hood in earnest'. The students' activities possibly could be dismissed as youthful pranks, but by coincidence, a few months later, the KKK claimed responsibility for burning down four shops in Mt Eden in Auckland.[9] The Klan appeared to have set up branches further south, such as in Christchurch, with glimpses of 'white sheeted night raiders on the Cashmere Hills'. Claims were made that the person behind this activity was an official from the Protestant Political Association, who claimed to be a 'minister (emeritus) of the Presbyterian Church'. Apparently the head of the KKK in New Zealand was 'Klansman White, the Grand Dragon of the invisible empire, New Zealand'.[10]

In 1923 Indians in Christchurch began to get a nasty taste of the white racism that would plague the city several years later. Two Indians who had recently moved there from Rotorua received a note under their door, warning, 'Beware! Ku Klux Klan is here; you are watched; warning!' Stones were also thrown at a shop on Colombo Street that was owned by Indians. The *New Zealand Herald* screamed, 'A WARNING TO HINDUS . . . the acts are the work of hoodlums, but it is borne in mind that one of the objects of the Klan is to make it impossible for Orientals to like New Zealand.'[11] Blatant racism could be deflected to foreign extremism or local thugs, but, as we will see, there were expressions of anti-Indian sentiment from far more respectable folk.

Hostility towards Indians intensified in New Zealand after World War I, as they were a scapegoat for economic problems, such as unemployment, housing shortages and low agricultural prices. Indians were visibly different and considered threatening to not only the economy but also the social and moral order. The presence of Indians and Chinese especially complicated the racial hierarchy and

Early settlers in Pukekohe, circa 1922–24. Front row from left: Makan Lala, Ramji Manga, Uka Chhiba, others unknown. Back row: Vallabh Kuvar, 'Govind', Magan Hari, Raman Kanji.

relations at Pukekohe, where Māori provided much of the seasonal labour for Pākehā potato farmers. Pukekohe was hardly isolated from global racist discourse. George Parvin, a British immigrant and secretary of the White New Zealand League, collected newspaper cuttings from South Africa, Canada, the United States and Australia on the 'Asiatic problem', and on eugenics and other 'scientific' racial theories.[12] In November 1925, the *Franklin Times* reported A. R. Hatt (formerly of the Defence Department), who asserted that while the prestige of the white race had slumped since the war, the 'teeming millions of the East' had applied President Woodrow Wilson's doctrine of self-determination. Although the white nations were recovering from their postwar exhaustion, 'the asiatics are taking advantage of the situation (look at Pukekohe Hill)'.[13]

The White New Zealand League was formed in Pukekohe in December 1925, one of its key aims being to enable local businessmen and landowners to push for 'legislation making it illegal to lease or sell land to Asiatics'.[14] The *Franklin Times* reported grossly exaggerated claims of 'large numbers of Asiatics' leasing land, an 'influx of Asiatics',[15] and an 'Asiatic invasion'[16] — hardly evident in the official figures (see table overleaf) — and the observation of J. J. Coady, a local business owner, that the 'influx of Asiatics is out of all proportion to the newcomers from the UK during the last six years'.[17] Still, the White New Zealand League wrote to Richard Bollard, the minister of internal affairs,[18] and lobbied for legislation to prevent further encroachment by Asians on the land or from buying shops, and the exclusion of further Asian immigration into New Zealand. Exclusion would also be at a personal level: 'We cannot have them [as] members of our social institutions, nor can they have a place in our homes as friends or guests.'

Support for the league came from the 'Franklin County Council, an authority vitally interested in the subject, since so much of its territory has been invaded by Asiatics'. The *Franklin Times* advocated that the

> only workable remedy . . . should be the privilege of any County or Borough Council to fix a quota of Asiatics that might be permitted to reside within its boundaries. There can be no possible excuse for permitting these people to ruin some of the most attractive neighbourhoods we have, and it is a villainous injustice to the residents that they should be allowed to invade the vicinity of their homes.[19]

Opposition to Indians leasing and buying land galvanised the White New Zealand League into existence, but it gained momentum through propaganda about the supposed moral, sexual and health threat posed by Indians. The league produced pamphlets containing images of dirty 'Hindu shacks' Indians were said to occupy.

'Races' of Franklin County and Pukekohe Borough

Year	European	Indian	Chinese	Others	Māori
1916	9535	1	5	29	399
1921	11,040	3	10	17	629
1926	12,264	17	30	15	767
1936	14,671	63	18	35	1169
1945	16,690	68	24	36	1675

Census of New Zealand, 1916–45. These figures include those of both full and mixed 'race'. The European figures include those classified as European/Māori 'quarter-caste' who were not included on the Māori census.

KEEP NEW ZEALAND WHITE !

This represents the latest style in a Residential Flat. The Hindus are noted for this type of dwelling, which is in striking contrast to the neat houses of the small settlers.

KEEP NEW ZEALAND WHITE !

One of Pukekohe's modern Farm Houses---Pukekohe has been noted for its intense cultivation, its productivity, its thrifty and industrious small farmers---Note the children, they represent the future citizens of the Dominion in the making, and the greatest asset the Empire has. Think of the environment. Protect them from its contaminating influence.

The White New Zealand League's propaganda in 1926 contrasted images of a temporary ramshackle tent claimed to be a typical Hindu dwelling with that of a 'neat' European farmhouse, with children sitting outside.

This White New Zealand League flyer, from 1926, highlighted the need to protect white children from the 'contaminating influence' of Asian migrants.

> As a rule 20 or 30 of these black men were huddled together in a shanty, something approaching an ordinary pig-sty, some sleeping standing up ready to start work in the morning. The white man could not possibly hope to compete with them under such conditions.[20]

Pukekohe's mayor, J. Routly, disputed that Indians (whom he called 'darkies') lived as poorly as people thought. He drew attention to the local camps where Māori lived, which were 'not very pleasant'. But George Parvin, ever upholding white privilege and economic exploitation, found those conditions acceptable because Māori were 'far different to the Asiatic races'.[21]

The supposed Asian influx was presented as a threat to the healthy white settler's standard of living. White children, 'the future citizens of the Dominion in the making, and the greatest asset the Empire has', should be protected from this 'contaminating influence'.[22] Although white rationale for excluding Indians from Pukekohe was localised within economics and morality, it was part of global discourse about the threat to white civilisation, as hinted at by the *Franklin Times*:

> The serious danger with which civilisation is threatened does not come from actual savages, or even from those of a little higher plane, who may be called barbarians. The peril is from those dark-skinned races which have long ago put on a thin veneer of semi-civilisation, but have remained for centuries without rising any higher — are really constitutionally incapable of rising any higher. No better example of this class of people can be found than the Hindus. Mentally and morally incapable of real civilisation they, many centuries ago, rose as high on the human plane as they had it in them to rise, and have remained stationary ever since . . .
>
> They come not as conquerors of untamed nature, but as hangers-on and parasites . . . as snappers-up

> of unconsidered trifles. Possessed of a fair amount of physical vigour and capacity for manual labour, their standard of living enables them to extract a living in conditions impossible to the white man. Their mental and moral attributes are as far apart from ours as the poles are asunder.[23]

When he disseminated the league's propaganda, Parvin passionately spread the fear that Asians would overrun the country. He made sure that newspapers, trade unions and local bodies throughout New Zealand received copies of the league's two booklets.[24] Recipients were requested to pass resolutions in support of the league, and to act as pressure groups 'to protect our own and the native race'. The editor of the *Auckland Star* found that 'the views expressed by the founders of the White New Zealand League are quite moderate and reasonable, and the questions that have been raised demand very serious attention from the general public as well as the Government'.[25]

Parvin claimed to have widespread support from the media, trade unions, retailers, growers, local bodies,[26] the RSA and the New Zealand Natives' Association. He established branches of the White New Zealand League in Wellington, warning growers in Lower Hutt and greengrocers and drapers in Wellington that 'Asiatics would get a hold and would crush out the white traders'.[27] The league reported that its Wellington branch, supported by 'commercial interests', had a commitment from government departments that they would deal with white fruiterers in preference to Asians.[28] It is uncertain whether this measure was enacted. Parvin also warned about the increasing number of 'Hindus' in Auckland; 'before long they would create a serious problem for the authorities unless something drastic was done to restrict their entry into New Zealand'.

The White New Zealand League lingered on during the economic depression of the late 1920s and early 1930s. In January 1929 Parvin was informed that 'a number of Hindus from Fiji were on their way to settle in New Zealand', so he 'immediately' telegraphed a protest to the prime minister, Sir Joseph Ward, and to the minister of customs. The league was 'watching the position as regards the Asiatic Influx, very carefully and as far as could be gathered, a number of Hindus who had entered New Zealand on a "short stay" permit were overstaying their term and appeared to be settling in the Dominion', partly because, according to Parvin, customs officers were not being vigilant about Indian immigration. These observations prompted the *Franklin Times* to ask if a white New Zealand would become 'pie-bald'.[29]

The league canvassed parliamentary candidates in 1928 to gauge support for its white New Zealand policy and to ascertain views on 'the subject of the silent penetration of Asiatics'. One proposal was that Asians should carry identification cards. 'New Zealand has legislative powers to keep out Asiatics, including Indians, and it rests with Cabinet to enforce it. The police are put to much trouble and expense in identifying individual Asiatics, and an identification certificate would obviate this.'[30] The *Franklin Times* reminded its readers that the league

> deserves the thanks of the community for its timely reminder that the most important question that New Zealand has before it has almost been lost to sight during the present election campaign. . . . the leaders of the parties have been so intent upon offering bribes to the electors, that they have forgotten that greatest matter of all, the preservation of the purity of our race . . . [Therefore] if we do not desire to see New Zealand ruined like Fiji and Natal and other parts of South Africa have been we must face these difficulties. It is far better to give some offence than to see the country economically injured and racially ruined.[31]

As will be seen in later chapters, the employment of Māori and white women by Indians provoked the ire of the White New Zealand League. Candidates in the 1928 elections were asked if they would support the league's policy that Asians should be prohibited from employing 'white and native girls'.[32] This suggestion was in line with the league's manifesto, which asserted that

> [t]he native race, together with our own, is intermingling with them, the result being a half-caste citizen of the future. . . . The warning note is sounded to be up and doing to protect civilisation from the rising tide of colour. . . . The doors of the Dominion must be bolted and barred against Asiatics.[33]

Māori women were considered particularly vulnerable to Indian men, provoking fears of a 'dilution of the race'. When D. S. Dale presented evidence in 1929 before the Committee to Investigate Conditions and Accommodation of Maoris Employed in European, Chinese and Asiatic Market Gardens in Auckland and Surrounding Districts, chaired by Sir Āpirana Ngata, he quoted Professor J. W. Gregory's *Menace of Colour* on the supposed evils of racial miscegenation:

> I would restrict them to the smallest possible amount. If the Chinese are allowed to settle extensively [in America] they must either, if they remain unmixed, form a sub-race in the position, if not of slaves, that of a class approaching to slaves, or if they mix, they must form a bad hybrid. In either case, supposing the immigration to be large, immense social miscegenation must arise and eventually social disorganisation.[34]

Parvin wrote to Andrew Ngawaka (Ānaru Iehu Ngāwaka) of the recently formed Te Akarana Maori Association,[35] promising support for a white New Zealand and the protection of 'both our races'

The White New Zealand League used letters to the editor and political lobbying to raise the spectre of large-scale Indian and Chinese migration through the late 1920s and early 1930s.

THE ALIEN IMMIGRATION.

In good old days that used to be
We sang a song at every spree
Britannia Always Rules the Waves
And Britons Never Shall be Slaves.
We did our trade with one another
And treated every Brit as brother.

But in these days of competition
We get a constant exhibition
Of how Zealandia rules the waves,
By letting in a lot of slaves,
Who working hard and living mean
Are coming in a constant stream.

These yellow dusky sons of Ham
Are not concerned the slightest damı
With fancy rules of arbitration,
And thought out scheme of legislation
Where every worker with his neighbour
Shall rest assured of decent labour,

And while we sing "God Save the King'
And think we are the only thing,
The alien builds his habitation
By meane of "peaceful penertation";
And notwithstanding scores of Diggers
The public buys its fruit from niggers.
When circumstances later suit,
The alien will not stop at fruit;
He'll try his "peaceful peneration,"
To change the colour of this nation,
And when you find this thing come true
We'' ave to lok fcr pastures new.

Franklin Times, 3 February 1926

REPATRIATION URGED

TO MAKE ROOM FOR WORKLESS

PETITION TO PARLIAMENT

Immediate repatriation of all Asiatics, particularly Chinese and Indians, in order that they may be replaced in their occupations by approximately 12,000 unemployed New Zealand workless men and boys is advocated in a petition presented to Parliament yesterday by Mr. J. N. Massey (Government, Franklin) on behalf of C. R. Lloyd and 1456 others.

It is stated that there are about 6000 Chinese and Indians in the Dominion, practically all of whom are working as market gardeners, hawkers, fruiterers, laundrymen, and market garden labourers, working about ten hours a day and seven days a week, depriving from work and livelihood nearly double the number of Europeans on ordinary working hours.

"The majority of them, the petitioners allege," are living in insanitary and immoral conditions, gravely endangering the future of our present fine Maori race. Evidence of this is unfortunately notorious, and has been frequently exposed. Both Chinese and Indians come to New Zealand to make money, and return with it to their native land, thus continuously weakening the finances of New Zealand.

Evening Post, 24 September 1932

LETTER FROM WHITE N.Z. LEAGUE.

TO A MAORI CHIEF.

The following letter has been sent by Mr G. T. Parvin, Hon. Sec. to the White New Zealand League, to Andrew Ngawaka, a Northern Maori chief, relating to a statement made to the Sun newspaper by Mr Ngawaka.

"I have read in the "Sun' of June 18 a statement made by you in regard to the contamination of your race by the Asiatics. It is not your good self that should be ashamed of this state of affairs that to those who take an active interest in the silent penetration of Asiatics into the affairs generally of the Dominion is so conspicuous.

"The people really concerned and who should be ashamed are the Government and the citizens of the Dominion generally. The White New Zealand League presented a petition signed by leading natives of Franklin protesting, as you are protesting now, against this co-habitating between the Indian and Chinese and the natives, and the free and easy mingling of both which is proving a menace to our civilisation and the purity of the race.

"The league was promised that immediate attention would be given the matter but nothing was done. The same state of affairs exists,I am sorry to say, between the whites and the Asiatics also, as police court proceedings have shown from time to time. This state of affairs points in no uncertain manner to the mongrelising not only of your own good race but also of our own.

Franklin Times, 21 June 1929

through forbidding Asians to employ 'native or white female labour'.

A White Producers' Cooperative Association was formed in Auckland in 1927. Race provided a simplistic explanation for the devastating economic depression that hit New Zealand during the late 1920s and early 1930s. Parvin claimed in 1930 that '[i]f all the Asiatics in the Dominion were deported tomorrow our unemployment would cease'.[36] He submitted a lengthy manifesto to local bodies, chambers of commerce and the RSA concerning Asians displacing European and Māori workers, especially in market gardening, but much play was made of moral issues, as Parvin asserted:

> That they are not good citizens and constitute a grave menace to any good environment as is instanced by the numerous major and minor crimes committed by them as reported from time to time in the daily press. That they live in gravely immoral surroundings and are a grave menace to the health and moral well-being of the whole of the Dominion . . . Differences in moral standards of the two races must ever be a source of social evil.[37]

In 1932, Jack Massey, Member of Parliament for Franklin, submitted a petition to Parliament from the White New Zealand League for the 'immediate repatriation of all Asiatics, particularly Chinese, and Indians, in order that they may be replaced in their occupations by approximately 12,000 unemployed New Zealand workless men and boys'.[38] This was an odd claim as, even by 1935, there were only about 3748 Indians and Chinese in the country, although the 1932 petition put the number at about 6000. Still, the petition claimed that the majority of Asians were

> living in insanitary and immoral conditions, gravely endangering the future of our present fine Maori race. The Asiatics of New Zealand are undesirables, being invariably of a low caste and class in their own country, and as

> such cannot be assimilated into our population, and are therefore of no economic value to the country.[39]

In the *Franklin Times*, 'Gleaner' wrote satirically that the 1932 petition was a 'hardy annual . . . Pomeranian-like yap of some of the good folk of Pukekohe', adding, 'No, our Pukekohe friends should admit the truth as they delightfully unconsciously admitted in their latest petition to Parliament — they are afraid of the Chinese and Indians because they work too hard. A little more of the old pioneering spirit and that fear would not exist.'[40]

Racial tension continued at Pukekohe long after the demise of the White New Zealand League. Scaremongering about the 'slow strangulation' of the white growers resurfaced at the 1937 annual meeting of the Franklin RSA. E. J. Campbell asserted that '[a]t present half the growers on Pukekohe Hill are Hindus, and within two years I predict the Hill will be black. I can assure you the position is serious and gives we white growers some grounds for concern.'[41] Parvin predicted that in a 'short time at the present rate of penetration, Asiatics would control the fruit and produce industries of the Dominion'. According to S. P. Day, who 'had watched the position carefully and had seen the ramifications of Asiatics', the competition was unfair because Asians were permitted to live under conditions that no white man could exist [*sic*].' Claims were made that 'Asiatics were scouring the district for land' and were able to offer higher prices than returned soldiers could.

Again the global context of the Asian 'danger' was invoked when a speaker referred to British Columbia, alleging that there was 'open warfare among Asiatics who had gained complete control of the market gardening, aerated waters, service stations and other industries. The position there was very alarming and would be the same here unless drastic action was taken.' So the delegates at the meeting in Franklin told the RSA's central office:

> This returned soldiers' association views with alarm the rapid influx of, and control of the market garden industry,

> by Asiatics. The livelihood of many returned soldiers and their families is in jeopardy and the gravity of the position is such that the Government should be urged to take steps immediately to restrict the activities of these people.[42]

During the 1950s, objections to Indians in Pukekohe resurfaced. Parvin still waved the race flag:

> If this business of Indians continually buying up property continues, New Zealand, before long, will find itself in much the same position as Fiji is today, where the Indian community is more or less in control. Why, Indians are arriving in this country in increasing numbers. I am informed that 50 per cent of the passengers by plane from Singapore are Indians. In Australia they are not allowed to land. What is good enough for Australia is good enough for us.[43]

Parvin's claims were dismissed by Pukekohe's mayor and by local Indian leaders. Yet the hostility in the 1950s at Pukekohe, while not widely supported, reflected attitudes that continued to ferment within New Zealand.

Kiwi-Indians did not accept the rise of white racist organisations. New Zealand Indian leaders, especially Jelal Natali and Inder Singh Randhawa, countered with several letters to newspapers.

A stronger and permanent response to discrimination against Indians was the amalgamation of the three Indian Associations based at Auckland, Wellington and Taumarunui to form the New Zealand Indian Central Association in 1926.

ASIATICS IN NEW ZEALAND.

(To the Editor.)

Sir,—"Puke's" reply to my letter is not very convincing. He seems very ignorant of the way Asiatics in general are living in New Zealand. I will invite him, whenever he is ready, at my own expense to come and visit some of the Asiatics' homes in New Zealand, when I am sure he will acknowledge that he is wrong in his conclusion. Of course, there are exceptions in all cases. At the same time I will take him to the houses of some Europeans who are living in worse conditions than the Asiatics, and who are not only tolerated but respected by the self-respecting white man. I know the Asiatics from the business people down to the hawker, and I can assure "Puke" that the standard of living of this people is not much lower than the average working-class Europeans. I do not understand how goods produced by Asiatics can be cheaper than those of Europeans in this country. As far as I can gather, all the produce goes to the mart and brings the price according to the quality, and irrespective of whether it was produced by Asiatics or Europeans. In fact, the Asiatic grown vegetables bring higher prices in most cases. It is very difficult to believe that the land is depreciating on account of Asiatic neighbours.—I am, etc.,

J. K. NATALI.

P.O. box 1623, Auckland.

Auckland Star, 6 January 1926

WHITE NEW ZEALAND.

(To the Editor.)

Sir,—I happened to read a pamphlet issued by the White New Zealand League. I rather think the league has done some service to the Indian community. If the supporters of the league care to read, I wish to remind them of the words of the great Queen Victoria, so that in their light they may weigh their own argument. It was Queen Victoria who said: "There shall not be in the eye of the law any distinction or disqualification whatever founded on mere distinction of colours, origin, language or creed, but the protection of the law in letter or substance shall be extended impartially to all alike." Has the league any respect for the above-mentioned words? If the league has the welfare of the British Empire at heart, then it can spend its money better in trying to strengthen the ties of the Empire by creating an atmosphere of goodwill rather than loosening it by creating racial discrimination. I believe the true citizens of New Zealand have not fo[illegible]ten Their regard for us is daily evidenced by civic receptions paid to our hockey representatives in every town wherever they go. I wonder i the white league will take any lesson out of it.—I am, etc.,

INDER SINGH RADHAWA.

Auckland Star, 8 June 1926

The Indian community responded to the White New Zealand League with its own letters to the editor, refuting the league's claims and pointing out that they, too, were equal citizens of the British Empire.

WHITE NEW ZEALAND.

(To the Editor.)

Sir,—Under the above heading a few articles have appeared in the Press but your long article of the 13th inst reached the culminating point in the unwholesome and ugly misrepresentation tactics employed by the handful of agitators who designate themselves members of the White New Zealand League. Their activities can only create disturbance and racial discrimination in this peaceful country, and can serve no useful purpose whatever, especially in view of the fact that their energies are based upon misrepresentations of facts. The Indians are British-born subjects belonging to the Aryan race and are therefore brothers and first cousins to the English people, and they demand their rightful place in the brotherhood of the British Commonwealth. The illustration in your article is the picture of a dirty shed which no longer exists and in which no Indian has ever resided. The shed was used as an occasional shelter for agriculturial implements, etc. for some time. Thus the suggestion that this shed is a type of Indian habitation is a gross misrepresentation. The adjoining corrugated iron shed was empty when your photo was taken; it has since been occupied by Maoris It is certainly true that an Indian slept in this iron shed for a few nights temporarily, while he was making permanent arrangements. But what about similar corrugated sheds that were used by the white settlers in Point Chevalier recently? Or is it more justifiable for a white person to live in such a place than it is for your "dusky" man? The White League have published a booklet in which the same illustration appears as well as the photo of another larger shed which was a wagon shed, but is now empty and has never been used as a house Why, then, this mischievous propaganda? Will India's sacrifices be forgotten and will a handful of mischief-makers thwart the prevailing goodwill and blind and prejudice the just-minded Christian citizens of peaceful New Zealand?—I am, etc.,

N.Z. INDIAN ASSOCIATION.

Auckland.

Auckland Star, 17 April 1926

New Zealand Indian Central Association: Early days

Delegates at the inaugural meeting in Taumarunui of the Country Section of the New Zealand Indian Central Association in 1926 decided to form a New Zealand Indian Association. Inder Singh Randhawa reported that the 'Pukekohe menace was a top subject in the debate. The words of Queen Victoria were once again recalled with *[sic]* condemn the present menace frankly offered against us by the selfish white people. The declaration of Queen Victoria is treated as null and void. She was Queen Victoria who said, "There shall not be in the eye of the law any distinction or disqualification whatever founded on mere distinction of colour, origin, language or creed but the protection of the law in letter or substance shall be extended impartially to all alike."

'The Indian Community notes with regret that these words of great honour are treated as a mere scrap of paper. It was argued at the meeting that Indians being the British subjects deserve all protection in the eye of the law as those of the whites. It was appreciated that equality is God's gift to human beings and this principal is as sacred to the Indians as souls to them.

'The White New Zealand League's action were wholeheartedly condemned as they are not in the right spirit. The White New Zealand League is issuing vague and misleading statements to cause misunderstandings in the minds of the peaceful New Zealanders to give growth to racial hatred was the opinion of every Indian attending the meeting.'

The meeting regarded it as of great importance to carry on a propaganda in face of the white N.Z. League to supply with correct information to the N.Z. public to promote good understandings. The Indian hearts were very sore on the point that there was a time when we threw our lot with the whites in the hour of need but now it [is] the time when we are regarded as unfit to live on their sides in times of peace. It was agreed upon that a man is known by his deeds. Justice and fairplay stand equally for the whites as well as the black. Different colour is due to living under different atmosphere. So a unanimous demand for forming [an] Association was created at the meeting.[44]

— *Country Section*, NZICA, 8 May 1926

Office-bearers of the New Zealand Indian Central Association, 8 October 1939. Standing from left: Banta Ram Singh (vice-president), Karam Singh Basi (treasurer), Kanjibhai Kevel Patel, Jelal K. Natali (president), Unkabhai K. Patel (secretary). In front: P. W. Lachpuria (auditor).

Inder Singh Randhawa, the New Zealand Indian Central Association's first general secretary, circa 1950s.

Sadanand Maharaj, from Fiji, was elected as NZICA's first president. He was the son of Badri Maharaj, the first Indo-Fijian member of Fiji's Legislative Council. Sadanand studied law at Auckland University in the 1920s before he worked as a solicitor. Inder Singh Randhawa became NZICA's general secretary. NZICA's constitution clearly stipulated the association's role to monitor proposed legislation that might affect Indians:

> To watch and consider proposed changes in law relating to Indians and to make representations to the authorities in connection with the existing law and any such proposed changes and to take such other steps in relation there to as may be expedient.[45]

NZICA also advocated restitution: 'To seek the redress of wrongs affecting the Indians in New Zealand.' The association would act in general, but not for individual cases of discrimination. NZICA presented a petition to Parliament in protest against the activities of the White New Zealand League. It is unclear if the petition was tabled, but Dr Baldev Singh Share led a deputation that met with Richard Bollard, minister of internal affairs, on 11 June 1926.

Bollard assured the deputation:

> You have been admitted here as British subjects and you have the same right to justice and protection as anybody else in the Dominion, and that justice and protection you will receive so long as you conform to the laws of the country . . . We will see that justice is done to you and that you have an opportunity of defending yourselves.[46]

Petition by New Zealand Indians: Protesting the actions of the White New Zealand League

'We, the undersigned British born Indian subjects, protest against the efforts of the White New Zealand League to create racial discrimination between His Majesty's Loyal subjects in peaceful New Zealand and most respectfully appeal to the New Zealand Government to safeguard the interests of the Indian community domiciled in the Dominion, who unflinchingly offered their lives and wealth for the victory of the British banner in the world war; despite our brown colour we are better for the future of the Empire than those white nations who have proved to be enemies of our great British Empire.'[47]

— NZICA petition, 1926

opposite: Part of the petition protesting the actions of the White New Zealand League against Indians in Pukekohe and other agricultural areas, signed by founding NZICA members, 1926.

We wish also to point out, Sir, that our main object in coming to you here is not to invite or encourage more immigration from India but to voice the aspiration of those who have been lawfully admitted into the Dominion and are domiciled as permanent residents of New Zealand. Time has proved that the Indians are the most law abiding persons and that they always have the best interest of the Empire at heart. Our feelings are greatly hurt when we find some of the supporters of the White League looking contemptuously at us and speaking ill of our Community. Such men have really no welfare of the Empire at heart and are only trying to damage the ties of our mutual bond. They really have got no substantial good at their hearts but are blinded by racial prejudice.

Prosperity of New Zealand depends mostly on Agriculture. Our people have proved themselves to be very helpful on the farms. The King Country, Waikato and Hauraki Plains are the visible proofs of our labour. A great bulk of our people have settled in the above districts and have become good settlers and we are proud to mention that the farmers of the above districts are well pleased with our behaviour, honest working and proper living.

In conclusion we sincerely hope that the Government of New Zealand will extend the same justice to us as has been done in the past and we respectfully urge upon the Government to safe-guard our interests in the future. We are here before you, sir, not to beg for mercy but to ask for justice and fairplay and we trust and believe our requests will be complied with.

We are,

Your Loyal Subjects,

B. B. Shah M.B., D.P.H., L.R.C.P. & S.E., &c.

Inder Singh Radhawa

Karm Singh

J. R. Kapoor.

S. M. Jahraj

Bunta R. Singh

J. K. Natali

four.

Discrimination at Work

Employment has been one of the main areas where Kiwi-Indians have faced discrimination: in obtaining work, promotions and appointments, and in purchasing land and businesses. White race organisations argued that competition from Asians in employment and business was a reason to restrict immigration.

Indian politician Srinivasa Sastri confirmed that Indians suffered racial prejudice in employment when he toured New Zealand as part of a mission to investigate the conditions of Indians in the white Dominions in 1922.[1] Discrimination, in both formal and covert forms, affected those in self-employment and in waged work. Calls to exclude Indians from the workplace were tied to immigration exclusion. Discrimination at work could be all-pervasive, affecting residence and accommodation. Although exclusionary demands to introduce legislation to restrict or exclude Indians from employment or property ownership surfaced, formal enactment of this agitation was rare, given that it would have been at odds with New Zealand's egalitarian ethos.

Indians, many of whom were Muslims or Sikhs, worked as hawkers throughout Aotearoa during the nineteenth and early twentieth centuries. These men were highly mobile, travelling by horse and selling goods such as textiles and clothing in both urban and remote areas.

By the late nineteenth century pressure groups and politicians in New Zealand, as in other white settler colonies, demanded racially exclusionary immigration policies. Spurred by fears of economic competition, and by exaggerated representations of the moral and sexual threat of Asians, there was an outcry in Parliament about itinerant 'Hindoo' hawkers during the 1890s.[2] (The term 'Hindoo' was applied to Indians of all religions and cultures, and conflated Indians with 'Assyrians', or Syrians and Lebanese.)

New Zealand's economic recession of the early 1890s also gave rise to strong agitation for the total exclusion of Asians and for restricting the movements of Asian residents. The Liberal Party, headed by Seddon and Reeves, invoked the 'Asiatic fear' through introducing the 1892 and 1894 Hawkers and Pedlars Bills, the 1896 Undesirable Hawkers Prevention Bill and the 1900 and 1901 Pedlars and Hawkers Bills. Aliens bills in 1892 and 1893, and the Undesirable Immigrants Exclusion Bill in 1894 also proposed restrictions on hawkers.

The 1896 Undesirable Hawkers Prevention Bill aimed to make it unlawful 'for any person to hold a license under this Act unless he is a British subject, or has been naturalized in the colony for not less than twelve months on the date on which the application for the license is lodged'.[3] When Seddon introduced the bill he cited that

> abuses had occurred which rendered it necessary that hawkers coming into the country should be a desirable and respectable class of persons. The country had been simply deluged for some time past with a class of hawkers whom it was not desirable to allow in the colony. They had been refused hawkers' licenses in New South Wales, and

above: Street hawkers, Wellington, 1926.

below: 'Bhoot Bungalow', 174 Tory Street, central Wellington, 1957.

> they came in large numbers to New Zealand, and were coming still. There ought to be power to regulate this important question.[4]

Thomas Mackenzie, member for Clutha, backed up Seddon. 'Indian hawkers sold the most worthless brummagem stuff imaginable, which otherwise would not come into these districts,' he claimed, noting that he had had 'reports from women of insolence on the part of the hawkers'.[5] But independent member of Parliament John Duthie wanted to see more evidence of these complaints.

All of these bills intended to restrict Indian hawkers from working in New Zealand failed to be passed and met resistance from the Legislative Council.

Indian hawkers eventually faced increasing regulation in Aotearoa's urban centres. In 1913 Auckland's mayor, Christopher Parr, refused to issue permits to the 'influx of Hindus who wanted licenses to hawk fruit', because they did not pay rent or rates. Indians were also denied permits during this period in Christchurch.[6] In August 1914, Francis Fisher, Member of Parliament for Wellington Central, stated: 'I have seen from personal observations they [the Hindus] are starting fruit-stalls. In some cases they are very close to European shops, and the men who are paying rent and taxes have these men underselling them. They are keeping their stalls up to date with acetylene lights, and carpets on the footpath, and making their competition very severe to those engaged in the trade. I think it is desirable to put a stop to this sort of thing.'[7]

After World War I, regulations were introduced to standardise fruit hawking in Wellington, covering the hawkers' character, as well as the maintenance of sanitary living conditions and the storage of fruit.[8] By 1918 Wellington City Council tried to refuse granting hawking licences to Indians, although regulations stated that all British subjects could apply.[9] Lalloo Morar told me that Indian hawkers were discriminated against through having to bid to hire fruit stands, but he did not recall white hawkers having to do this.[10]

Indar Singh: Hawker

'A striking and colourful personality who was well-known in the Waikato during the first decade of the present [twentieth] century was an Indian hawker named Indar Singh, who travelled around the district hawking his clothing and goods, and offering them for sale at Maori huis and European fairs.

'Whenever there was a hui or Maori gathering of any size Indar Singh would arrive, his goods piled high on two packhorses. No one could throw a "diamond hitch" with more dexterity than he could. Even in those days few people knew the art of arranging the packing rope like an inverse diamond with its simple central knot so placed that the four "spiders" would encompass the load.

'Timing his visit to a nicety, Indar Singh would arrive at the gathering two days before hand. He would off-load under some convenient tree, and lay out his wares before the eyes of all and sundry. He was in no haste to do business, but in the art of display Indar Singh was a past master. He knew the psychological effect of folding red blankets, rainbow-hued scarves, yellow and black check trousers and pink silk blouses in such a manner as to arouse the interest and covetousness of prospective purchasers. After viewing the goods, the people would disperse and they could be depended upon to return later with the money with which to acquire the goods they coveted.

'Indar Singh always declined to sleep in the thatched huts in which he was offered accommodation for his stay. Making some religious excuse for declining the invitations, he would hobble his horses, and covering his goods with a tarpaulin neatly pegged down, he would stretch himself out on top and go to sleep in his own blankets.

'A busy day of trade would follow, and there was sure to be many envious eyes cast on the handsome young natives attired in their newly purchased loud check trousers, and still louder yellow waistcoats striding around. Indar Singh was never in evidence at the actual time, however, for he invariably withdrew just prior to the event and went on his way.

'The Indian was a high-caste Sikh. His hair and beard were never cut. His beard was parted at the chin and plaited, the two plaits passed upward behind his ears and secured under the folds of his turban.'[11]

— *Waikato Times*, 5 February 1960

Hira Bava, standing
in front of the
Caledonian Hotel,
Basin Reserve,
Wellington, 1948.

WHY THE BARROWS WERE ALLOWED.

Councillor Meadowcroft said that the council had laid it down definitely that the terms of licence had to be strictly observed, that ground space could not be used, what fruit might be exposed (as oranges or bananas, which were peeled before being eaten) and so on. The reason why the Asiatics were allowed upon Wellington streets was that Wellington people had thought that the whites were keeping the prices too high and that with Asiatic competition prices would be more reasonable, but that was a mistake.

A member of the deputation: "Then why carry it on?"

The City Solicitor said that the council had full power under the Municipal Corporations Act either to permit or stop the sale of fruit from barrows.

Mr. P. Braithwaite, secretary of the Retail Shopkeepers' Association, said that he saw no reason for the barrows at all; the policy was really one of bringing the European down to the level of the Asiatic. The Retailers' Association was opposed to the barrow system altogether.

Evening Post, 27 January 1932

Indian fruit and vegetable sellers faced continual attempts by councils and retailers' associations to prevent them from plying their trade.

Despite such attempts at restriction, Indians supplied fruit and vegetables to many towns and cities in the North Island and in Christchurch. Indian hawkers and shopkeepers had a valuable role in bringing goods to Māori living in remote rural communities. For example, during the 1920s, Santa Singh sold goods to Māori labourers who were breaking in the railway line from Gisborne to Tāneatua in the Bay of Plenty. He also took goods by packhorse up into the Ureweras at Maungapōhatu, to Rua Kēnana, the Tūhoe prophet. After Ibrahim Musa arrived in New Zealand in 1925 he opened a general store on Matakana Island, where most of his customers were Māori.

B. V. Chhiba (left) at M. Budhia's bottle-collection depot, Christchurch, 1967.

Collecting bottles and other recyclable waste products, such as scrap metal, rags and bones, was an essential service and important occupation for some Kiwi-Indians, but again it was one where they faced discrimination. In 1927 Wellington City Council passed a by-law requiring Indian bottle collectors to wear an identification strap on their sleeves.[12] It was an amendment to a 1908 by-law that dealt with the licensing and the conduct of hawkers, pedlars and keepers of coffee or other street stalls. Section 2 (iii) stated:

> Every Household Refuse Purchaser shall whilst in the exercise and pursuance of his said business or calling carry his license with him and shall show the same to any police constable or officer of the Council who shall demand the same and shall in addition at all times have affixed to his right arm a metal plate inscribed 'W.C.C. Licensed Household Refuse Purchaser' and having inscribed thereon also the number of the license issued to the bearer.[13]

The Wellington Indian Association met with the council, which amended the by-law to stipulate a small bottle collectors' badge instead of an armband. In 1943, under the leadership of the NZICA president, Ganda Nager, 26 Indians formed the Wellington Indian Bottle Dealers and Waste Products Association, to protect the interests of Indian bottle collectors. Indians in Christchurch formed a similar organisation in 1943: the Waste Products and Bottle Dealers Association. By 1948 there were approximately 20 bottle recyclers in Christchurch, most of whom were Indian.

Indians in New Zealand faced hostility when they were seen to be taking jobs from Pākehā. In 1913 objections were raised in

Parliament that white men had been made redundant because Indians were employed within the private and public sectors. Prime Minister Bill Massey demanded the 'services of coolies' employed by the State Forestry Department at Rotorua be terminated.[14] As noted, anger and fears about Indians taking jobs from returned servicemen increased after World War I, especially amidst unemployment and a depressed economy. The RSA led anti-Asian xenophobia, claiming to be protecting jobs for white New Zealanders. Even the Soldiers Mothers' League pressured the prime minister to 'boycott all trade carried on by Indians'.[15] Several trade unions added to the clamour, including the Furniture Trade Industrial Union of Workers, the Grocer Assistants' Union, and the Timber Workers' Union. The Waterside Workers' Union passed a resolution refusing to work the cargo on vessels landing 'Hindus' and Chinese at Auckland.

Although the RSA claimed that its white New Zealand policy was supported by all trade unions in New Zealand,[16] this conflicted with organised labour's principle to support oppressed workers, regardless of race, who were exploited by 'unprincipled commercialism'.[17] Harry Holland, leader of the Labour Party, editor of the *Maoriland Worker* and the member for Buller, was concerned about the Immigration Restriction Bill. He hoped that 'the legislation of New Zealand shall be framed so as to protect the standards of life of the people of New Zealand, and especially the working-people, but that it shall be framed also so as to protect the coloured immigrants who might be brought here, as they have been taken to other places for specific purposes'.[18] *Maoriland Worker* criticised unions who excluded 'coloured aliens', as union membership was a way to control any fears of Asians lowering wage rates or the standard of living. 'Labour should know no race, colour, or creed.'[19]

In 1920 there was an outcry when the Public Works Department hired five Indians to work on the construction of Evans Pass Road between Lyttelton and Sumner near Christchurch. The other workers downed tools, refused to work with 'black' labour and accused the Indians of accepting below-average rates. In fact

above: King Country scrubcutters Joala Singh Belling and others outside their hut.

below: Indian crewmen aboard the SS *Mongolia*, Auckland, 30 November 1910.

The Free Lance

An Illustrated Journal of Information and Racy Comment upon Topics of the Hour.

VOL. XIX.—No. 1041. WEDNESDAY, JUNE 9, 1920. SIXPENCE.

WILL IT COME TO THIS?

Free Lance, 9 June 1920

Cartoon by Tom Glover Ellis, depicting the hostility from the Returned Soldiers' Association and the Watersiders' Union to Indians and Chinese, seen to be usurping the rightful place of 'New Zealanders'.

the Indian workers' pay sheets showed that in their last job — in railway construction in the North Island — they had earned above the average rate.[20] The Waterside Worker's Union held a special meeting over the Evans Pass stand-off; 'sympathetic action would follow if the Hindus were not removed'.

The RSA also led protests when 38 Indians were hired by the Public Works Department to do road work in Wairarapa at Manawa Station near Tinui in 1920.[21] A meeting at Tinui agreed to send 'a vigorous protest' to the local member of Parliament, objecting to employing Hindus on public works. Indians hit back against the erroneous claims that they worked for below-award wages. In 1921 Indar Singh Purihar, Tiparchand, Gangu, Parema, and Hukam Singh submitted 'The Hindu Manifesto' to the Indian Overseas' Association, stating that it was 'incorrect that the average Hindu bush cutter works on less than the statutory or white man's standard wage'.[22]

Kiwi-Indians also reported covert discrimination in the workplace besides the public outcry that arose between the wars. Prominent Kiwi-Indian Jelal Natali had been a clerk in Gujarat, but could not obtain similar employment in New Zealand. Instead, he initially worked as a kitchen assistant in a boarding house:

> [O]ffice jobs for a coloured man at that time in 1920 were out of the question so I took a job as a kitchenman . . . Washing pots and pans, peeling potatoes and scrubbing floors was a bit hard and a 'come down' from an office job I had been used to, but I had no other choice.[23]

Chhotu Jivanji, a founder of the Auckland Indian Association, managed to be hired as a shipping clerk before 1920. But when white

'A scandalous policy'

'New Zealand is suffering at the present time from something approaching what might be called a Hindu invasion. The principal cities and towns in the Dominion are being flooded with Hindus, who are making desperate efforts to capture certain trades. The Asiatic element is very numerous in Wellington — in fact, the capital city's fruit trade is in the hands of the Chinese and Hindus. The Hindu is a danger to European women and children even when following the occupation of fruiterer, hawker, or "bottle merchant". But when we find the Education Department quite agreeable to the employment of Hindus as teachers in our schools, we cannot find words strong enough to condemn the Department's fatuous attitude. Apparently the Department is quite out of touch with the duties that are required of it. It is astounding to find that our Education Department is favourable to the introduction of the Hindu among our school children. Those officials of the Education Department who are responsible for this policy are in the wrong country — they should be in Russia.'[24]

— *Wairarapa Daily Times*, 7 April 1921

people refused to work in positions below him and threatened to go on strike, he resigned rather than attract attention. In schools, Indians could face opposition from white parents. A 'Hindu teacher' was to have been appointed at Tuakau school in Franklin District — the region that became the heartland of the White New Zealand League. At an annual general meeting in 1921 the good parents of Whangarata made it clear they were opposed to this appointment.[25]

Manilal Maganlal, born in Baroda, was a prominent lawyer in Mauritius and Fiji. He was unable to gain admittance to the legal 'Bar' in New Zealand. This rejection by the New Zealand Law Society was not just due to race, but also because he and his wife, Jehi Behn, were leaders in a sugar workers' strike in Fiji in 1920. The family had to leave New Zealand.[26]

We have seen that growers in Pukekohe were incensed when Indians took up market gardening. Indians were posed as an economic threat but their supposed 'immorality' was equally invoked. Thus Indians were entangled in an investigation into the poor working and living conditions of Māori agricultural labourers.

In 1929 Sir Āpirana Ngata headed the Committee to Investigate Conditions and Accommodation of Maoris Employed in European, Chinese and Asiatic Market Gardens in Auckland and Surrounding Districts.[27] The alleged immorality of Indians and Chinese came under scrutiny when the Ngata Committee was charged to investigate 'whether it is in the interests of public morality that the employment of Maori girls and women by Chinese and Hindus should be permitted to take place'. Racial contamination was seen to weaken both morality and the economy:

> The indiscriminate intermingling of the lower types of the races i.e., Maoris, Chinese, and Hindus will, in the opinion of the Committee, have an effect that must eventually cause deterioration not only in the family and national life of the Maori race, but also in the national life of this country, by the introduction of a hybrid race, the successful absorption of which is problematical . . . The intermingling of Maoris with the lower type of Chinese or Hindus, whether legally married or not, will have the effect of lowering the standard of living . . . The moral aspect is one that must also be taken into

> consideration under the present conditions, brought about by economic stress, and to some extent by the improvidence of the Maoris affected, the employment of Maori females by Chinese, who are deprived of the right to bring their own women into this country, and Hindus, and the indiscriminate intermingling of the sexes such as now obtains, must be viewed with alarm as tending to inevitably lead to immorality.[28]

The committee recommended that Māori females aged under 21 be prohibited from employment in market gardens controlled by Asians, unless under approved supervision.

The Ngata Committee also received complaints about economic competition from Indians — supposedly undercutting Europeans through working longer hours, accepting lower pay rates, and maintaining a lower standard of living than Europeans. 'The Hindu would have much lower expenses — no taxes and no family to keep.'[29] Business scruples, land values and immorality were clearly conflated in a farmer's submission to the Ngata Committee. He complained not only about the lack of cooperation by Hindus with local growers over exporting onions, but also that '[t]he Hindus have depreciated the value of my property so that I cannot sell it. Our children are not safe coming home from school.'[30]

Growers continued to protest about the 'Asiatic invasion' on market gardens in Franklin District and in Ohakune.[31] In 1937 a deputation of produce growers and fruiterers in Pukekohe and Auckland met the minister of labour, Tim Armstrong, to discuss allegations that Asians were evading labour legislation by not paying the same wages to workers as Europeans did. The solution put by the growers' association was to repatriate Asians — but 'Hindus', who were British subjects, could not be 'dealt with so easily' as Chinese. E. J. Campbell, the association's secretary, advocated that 'further immigration by Asiatics should be stopped and their activities restricted by a system of personal registration and licensing'.

The RSA's Auckland branch complained after World War I that

Dr Baldev Singh Share: Wrongfully convicted?

Baldev Singh, born in Lahore on 1 January 1883, was the son of Giani Ditt Singh, an intellectual and prominent Sikh politician with the Singh Sabha movement that aimed to reform Sikhism and advocate for Sikhs with the British. Having graduated with several medical qualifications in Europe, Baldev Singh secured medical registration in the United Kingdom in 1910, and later in New Zealand in 1921 and Fiji in 1928. In 1920 he emigrated to New Zealand with his wife, Cynthia Satwanti Share, a teacher and a nurse, their son Napoleon Delaware Share (Diliwar N. Singh), and his mother, who had been a college teacher in India, with the 'intention to make their home in New Zealand'.[32]

On 17 December 1920 Baldev Singh changed his name by deed poll to Baldev Singh Share, and by 1929 he had acquired New Zealand citizenship. A prominent spokesperson for the Indian community, he was at the forefront of the welcome in 1922 for Sastri, and in 1926 led the delegation to the minister of internal affairs to protest about the White New Zealand League.

But Share's career ended in shame when he was charged in 1929 after a 28-year-old-woman alleged that Share had indecently assaulted her. Historian Hew McLeod, who sifted through the ambiguous testimony, asked, 'Why was the case brought against Dr Share, and why did the jury find him guilty on such unconvincing evidence?' One of Share's friends alleged that a vindictive medical rival was behind the claims. Share did admit possessing 'rude pictures', but McLeod suggests that his conviction may have 'reflected attitudes developed or strengthened by the recent controversy concerning Indian immigration. The jury was composed entirely of Europeans and the trial was held in the shadow of the White New Zealand League's unsavoury campaign to have Indians repatriated. Once again, however, we are unable to offer a definitive explanation. All one can say is that in retrospect it is inconceivable that Dr Share would be charged, much less convicted, if evidence of this kind were to be offered today.'[33]

Share was sentenced to two years in prison and his wife and son were left destitute. He was deregistered from practising medicine and their house was repossessed. The son died aged 19 after contracting tuberculosis. On 2 December 1931 Share was released on probation and returned to India two days later.

white men, especially returned soldiers, had no chance of success in the fruit business if they had to compete with Hindus. Returned soldiers were instructed to boycott Asian retailers. In 1920, the RSA demanded that Asians be prevented from securing contracts from government departments. This action followed a returned serviceman losing the tender, to a Chinese supplier, to supply vegetables to King George Hospital at Rotorua.[34] The RSA's Auckland branch submitted a remit about the Asiatic influx and Indians in the fruit business to the RSA's national conference in 1920. 'Mr. L. J. Garmson said that . . . [i]f the influx went on, as it was going New Zealand would soon be a second India.'[35]

In 1930 the New Zealand Fruit and Produce Auctioneers and Importers' Federation requested that the acting prime minister, minister of internal affairs, minister of customs, comptroller of customs and commissioner of police introduce legislation to address 'the present unsatisfactory trading methods of Asiatics'. The federation insisted that Asians should only trade under their 'correct names' and not different names.[36] Support for this measure also came from the White New Zealand League. Apparently using different names enabled a trader to declare bankruptcy or abscond and set up a business again in another town, or in the same city. The Fruit and Produce Auctioneers and Importers' Federation sought the compulsory registration of all Asians, whereby the police and firms they transacted business with were notified of any change in business or residence. In fact the practice of trading under different names was not confined to Asian traders; as, Indians sometimes adopted European names to avoid racism.[37] But the federation singled out Asian retailers to come under restrictive legislation and surveillance.

Again in 1936 the Fruit Marketing Committee appointed by the minister of industries and commerce came up with another racist solution to address 'Asiatic competition'. The committee proposed that it should be compulsory for Asian fruiterers to have their thumbprints registered.[38] Natali telegraphed Peter Fraser, the acting prime minister, urging a response on the 'British fair play line':

> This meeting of the Auckland branch of the New Zealand Indian Association views with grave concern the thumb-prints recommendation made by the Fruit and Vegetable Committee for all Asiatics engaged in the fruit and vegetable trade. If put into operation, this unjust recommendation will be most humiliating to our nationals, and we have not the slightest doubt that the fair-minded legislators of this wonderful Dominion will not pay any serious attention to this un-British suggestion.[39]

Fraser sympathised with the Indian Association's concerns. He insisted no slight was intended, and assured that government would 'not be party to any unjust discrimination against Indian citizens in New Zealand'.[40] The humiliating thumbprint regulation did not go ahead. But as we will see, the Auckland Retail Fruiterers' Association still tried to assert dominance over Indian retailers during World War II.

Today many drivers within Aotearoa's transport industry are of Indian descent. Indians such as Parbhu Deva in Auckland began driving and owning taxis there in the 1940s. Although the numbers of Indian drivers were then small, the Checker and Atta taxi companies objected at a meeting of the Auckland Metropolitan Licensing Authority in April 1942 to Indians being granted taxi licences. Samuel Coleman of the Auckland Retail Fruiterers' Association claimed that there would be 'a lowering in the standard of hours and conditions because of Asiatic competition', because this had occurred in the fruit retail trade. Returned servicemen, 'after serving their country . . . may come back and find Hindus running the taxi service'.[44] In 1961 two Indians in Wellington were

Shires Fruit & Vege Market: A family business

Shires Fruit & Vege Market, still operating today, is one of the longest-established ongoing retail fruit and vegetable businesses in New Zealand, as its website explains:

'It was by accident that Mr. Chhibabhai Pancha Patel first arrived in Dannevirke around 1922. He had left India, bound for Fiji in 1917 and somehow ended up in New Zealand. His journey of chance continued, travelling to Wairoa to look at business prospects when he happened to get off the train at Dannevirke. There he spotted a bookshop that was soon to become vacant, contacted the Wellington owner and within a short time, started what is now one of Dannevirke's longest established businesses.

'Shires was the first specialist fruit and vegetable shop in the Southern Hawke's Bay region. Chhibabhai took up the name Bill Shire when he arrived in New Zealand and subsequently named his business W. Shire & Co., the word 'shire' meaning county. It was at this time there was considerable anti-Asian feeling rife in New Zealand and it was advantageous to trade under a European name. Over the years the name changed to W. Shire & Son, and since 1990 [the business] has traded as Shires Fruit & Vege Market.

'There were no provincial markets in the early days . . . This meant a Sunday-night train journey to Wellington to buy at the Monday market; then catching the overnight train to Auckland to buy fruit such as bananas and oranges. Then back to Wellington for the Thursday market and finally, late on Friday, back home to Dannevirke, all while making arrangements for all his purchases to be freighted back to Dannevirke by rail. Then, it was Monday again and the routine continued. Chhibabhai also bought stock for his four shops on these trips which were located in Wairoa, Levin, Waipukurau and Taihape, which also traded under the name W. Shire and Company.'[41]

Chhibabhai's eldest son, Chunilal, was born in 1927, and by

Chunilal Patel, photographed here in 1974 at Shires Fruit & Vege Market.

1944 was part of the enterprise. Chunilal drove the big truck through to the markets twice a week in Palmerston North and once a week in Hastings. Chunilal recalled, 'We had a staff of 11 adult men working in the shop at that time and all the staff that manned the three shops were from my father's village in India; he was one of the first Indians to settle in Dannevirke'.[42]

Chunilal and his wife, Shantiben, had a family of nine children. Their sons, Peter, Suresh and Arvind, and Suresh's wife Nayna are still active in the business today. Chunilal's son Paul Patel, who heads an architectural firm in Palmerston North, is the current president of NZICA.

R. C. Hari: Speaking out about the 'Asiatic land grab' during World War II

Ravji Chhanna Hari (known as R. C. Hari) and his brother began to lease land on the slopes of Pukekohe Hill during the 1930s. Ravjibhai became secretary of the Pukekohe Indian Association, and in 1943 he wrote a letter to the editor of the *Franklin Times* when the Franklin RSA raised alarm at Asians buying land. One report had claimed that 'before Christmas, one Hindu owned 20 acres of Pukekohe Hill land, but Hindus now own something like 450 acres. This is not a correct statement, it is misleading and far from true. Before Christmas — one Hindu owned 50 acres of Pukekohe land and another Hindu owned 20 acres on Pukekohe Hill. Since then Indians have acquired 155 acres, but only a portion of this is on Pukekohe Hill. Chinese have bought 40 acres, a total of 195 acres bought by other than Europeans in the whole Pukekohe district, not Pukekohe Hill. The land owned by Indians is less than an average of 5 acres for each Indian grower. The Pukekohe Indian Association protests against loose statements against the Indians. The Indian growers are producing for the war effort as well as for civilian needs. They are working land some of which was not producing vegetables before. They buy only such land as is for sale, at fair prices to the seller, whether Europeans or not (where there is a sale there must be a seller). They have been leasing land for years at high rentals. They are British subjects. They are hard workers, and hard work is now required. If a restriction should be placed, it should apply to everybody, not only to Indians and Chinese.'[43]

refused membership of the Taxi Owners' Union. NZICA objected to this on the grounds of racial discrimination. The Federation of Labour and the Drivers' Union tried to rectify the issue.[45] Wellington City Council had also refused to employ Indian bus drivers in 1956. The Wellington Indian Association negotiated with the council so that employees were hired on their ability rather than race.[46]

Indian farmers continued to face obstacles in obtaining and renewing leases or purchasing property. Natali's attempts to acquire land in the King Country were rejected because 'he was not a farmer himself and he was not a suitable man to own property such as this'.[47] At the RSA's national conference in 1943, there were attempts to debar Asians and southern Irish (along with conscientious objectors and military defaulters) from purchasing land or houses until the returned servicemen from World War II were rehabilitated.[48] H. H. S. Westmacolt, from the Ōtorohanga RSA, argued that 'Asiatics' should be included in this ban because recently Hindus had been financed by a bank to buy some of the best land in that district before returned soldiers could do so. He claimed that these Indians were of the 'non-fight-caste; [but] there was no feeling against the Sikhs in the district'.

L. C. Logan from the Franklin RSA also wanted Asians excluded from purchasing further land because of their recent land acquisitions at Pukekohe. A lone voice, D. W. Russell from Christchurch, objected to this 'absurd' proposal, pointing out that Indians had fought with New Zealanders in Tunisia. The Pukekohe Indian Association publicly corrected misleading information about Asians suddenly acquiring land during the war.

Even after World War II, the race card continued to be dealt in Franklin district. In 1952, the Federated Farmers of Franklin

Unkabhai Kanji Dhanjee and Sushila Dhanjee in 1950. They provided a taxi service, and operated a general store at Murupara during the 1950s.

demanded that Asians' land be confiscated and that Asians should be repatriated.[49] Meanwhile, racist letters were sent to the minister of immigration: 'They are as thick as flies in Pukekohe and they are getting control of all the good land and creeping into businesses in town, they breed like flies and in time to come will join up with the Maori and cause trouble.'[50]

Until the late 1950s growers in Franklin District were also organised along racial lines, with separate organisations for Europeans, Chinese and Indians. The need for a common front (and common sense) succumbed to market pressures. Non-Europeans were invited to join the Franklin Growers' Association (formerly for whites only), and to hold office.

five.

War and Welfare

Kiwi-Indians have experienced a contradictory and often exclusionary relationship with the nation state in New Zealand. Two areas that have been neglected in the country's history are Indians and the military, despite the willingness of many Kiwi-Indians to serve in combat for New Zealand, and their eligibility for social welfare. Kiwi-Indians also faced discrimination when it came to making provisions for privately supporting their families in India and through insurance policies in New Zealand.

A reason given for denying Indians the same rights as white New Zealanders was the popular assumption that Indians had not served the nation during World War I. Instead, returned soldiers argued that Asians 'certainly were working to the detriment of the men who had left these shores to uphold the traditions of the Empire'.[1] Such claims disregarded the supreme sacrifice made by Indians to the empire: one million Indian troops fought overseas, at least 74,187 of whom gave their lives. These claims also overlooked the fact that most Indians were denied active duty in the military because they were not considered to be 'natural-born' British subjects, but neither were they 'aliens'; 'instead they were placed to some in-between space by the New Zealand government.'[2]

The New Zealand military establishment's attitude towards Indians played a significant role, too. Major General Alfred Robin,

Robert Ramchurn Soman (in uniform) and siblings, circa 1914. Soman had Indian ancestry but because he had a European mother he was able to serve in the military during World War I.

New Zealand's military commandant, did not want Indians serving within the New Zealand Expeditionary Force or in the reserve. Robin cited the vegetarian or halal dietary requirements of many Indians, and other restrictions proscribed by caste and religion: in military speak, 'commissariat difficulties'. Robin also queried Indians' capacity for hard military labour, and their physical condition. This was nonsense as many Indians had been recruited for arduous work throughout the empire or laboured in tough and remote conditions in Aotearoa. Moreover, there was a long and proud military tradition in India, especially among Sikhs. But Robin claimed that Indians were not suited to a European climate or for service with Europeans. In contradiction to this stance, he argued that labourers (including Indians) were still urgently needed in New Zealand.

Further evidence of an exclusionary policy towards Indians came from the adjutant-general, who advised the Recruiting Board to give indefinite leave to Indian recruits if balloted under the 1916 Military Service Act; decisions about such enlistment should be adjourned *sine die* (to another day).[3] Defence districts in New Zealand were instructed that their 'officers treat this as confidential as far as [the] public press is concerned and foregoing instructions do not apply to Maoris'.[4] The army, however, did not usually reject Indians who could trace British descent (usually from their fathers). Twenty-two young Anglo-Indian men, originally from St Andrew's Colonial Homes in Kalimpong, served in the NZEF during World War I.[5]

A few Indians who did serve in the New Zealand military had previous military experience in India or volunteered before the Military Service Act was passed in August 1916. Before emigration to New Zealand in 1892, Weer Singh Gill had served in the British army forces in China.[6] By 1894 he was working in Pipiriki, Taranaki. Weer Singh enlisted with the New Zealand army on 7 March 1916 at Trentham, where he served as a cook, but was discharged from the army three months later. Thirty-eight-year-old Sham Singh, another Punjabi immigrant, who had been a labourer in Wellington, also enlisted in March 1916.[7] He was transferred to the Māori

Contingent, 4th Rarotongan Company, only to serve for one month before being discharged on medical grounds. This didn't stop Sham from re-enlisting with the army on 11 April 1918.

Some Gujaratis living in New Zealand also enlisted during World War I, but did not serve overseas. These included Chhiba Dayal, from Karadi, who died during the 1918–19 influenza pandemic.[8] Gujarati Muslim Ismail Bhikoo was called up as a reservist in Auckland.[9] Ironically, although 'commissariat difficulties' were used as a pretext for excluding Indians in New Zealand from the army, some worked as cooks, such as Sukha Parsot and Bir Singh Gill.

Not all Kiwi-Indians accepted the army's 'systematic racial and religious intolerance towards Indian volunteers.[10] On 24 October 1916, Khushi Ram Kapoor complained after being rejected from military service. Kapoor, a railway worker in India, had arrived in New Zealand in 1909. He and his two brothers went on to own a sawmill and a general store at Taringamotu, near Taumarunui. Recruitment officials told Kapoor that the regulations meant that Fijians, Niueans and 'Hindoos' could not be accepted in the army. It seems that his pleas and case were partly brushed aside because he was considered to be 'somewhat under the influence of alcohol'.[11] Kapoor tried to send a telegram of protest to the British prime minister, H. H. Asquith, and publish a copy of this in the *New Zealand Herald,* to report that 'Recruiting Officer Auckland says Indians are undesirable for front'. Kapoor's actions were blocked by the censor. He stayed on in Aotearoa, where he died in 1952.

The Indians from Fiji who enlisted in the New Zealand army were usually assigned to the Māori Contingent.[12] For example, Jamal Khan (Taj Mahomed Khan), originally from Punjab, served with the police in Fiji before working in a bottle yard in Wellington. He enlisted twice, but because he suffered from rheumatism he did not take up active service. Khan died in 1918 during the influenza epidemic. Joe Abdul Rashid, a baker from Suva, and Anthony Vincent Grant, a law clerk from Fiji, were in the Māori Contingent, but were discharged because they also had rheumatism.

Despite the ridiculous exclusion of Kiwi-Indians who were

Indian soldiers hauling a mounted gun on Walkers Ridge, Gallipoli, Turkey, 1915.

Sham Singh enlisted in the New Zealand army in 1916 but only served for one month before being discharged. His photo is from his alien re-entry certificate.

'Soldier Singh': Decorated war hero

Jagt Singh, a trooper with the New Zealand Mounted Rifles, was decorated with the British War Medal, the Victory Medal and the 1914–15 Star for bravery in the Dardanelles Campaign.[13] His commanding officer, Lieutenant Colonel James McCarroll, praised Jagt for his 'quick thinking and helpfulness in the field':

'The Regiment H.Q. reached a small knoll and we dismounted and had a look and here was the whole Turkish force on the move back – we were within a hundred yards of them, so I ordered all to retrieve to the horse mount and get back. I could not find my horse and I saw the Turks on the hill and we got some heavy fire. I was running back, bullets flopping round me, so I fell behind a bush, then Jagt Singh came up with my horse. I can tell you I got mounted in record time. We retired and assembled about half a mile away.'[14]

Before emigrating to New Zealand in 1913, aged 24, Jagt had served in the cavalry in India for nearly six years with the 20th Deccan Horse. He enlisted in the New Zealand army in December 1914 and entered Trentham Camp the following month. He had been working as a sawmill hand in Masterton. 'Soldier Singh', as he was nicknamed, was first posted to Egypt with the Wellington Mounted Rifles, 3rd Reinforcements. In August 1915 at the battle of Chunuk Bair on Gallipoli, he was seriously wounded in the lower part of his body. After recovering, he rejoined his unit in Palestine and Egypt and then was transferred to the Auckland Mounted Rifles with the 4th Reinforcements. After the war, Jagt was discharged, having served with the army for four and a half years. He returned to New Zealand, although, like many pioneer Kiwi-Indians, he also had a home in India, making several trips between the two countries.

Jagt Singh, photograph from his certificate of registration, 1921.

Ratan Chand Mehra: Killed in action

Ratan Chand Mehra was posthumously awarded the British War Medal and the Victory Medal. Ratan, a Hindu from Lahore, Punjab, had earlier emigrated to New Zealand, where he worked as a labourer and Indian interpreter for John Maher at Taumarunui. He enlisted in the New Zealand army as a rifleman in the 4th Battalion, B Company at Trentham on 12 October 1915 and on 15 March 1916 reached Suez. He became the battalion's cook and was transferred to 1st Battalion A Company.

In December 1916 Ratan was admitted to the New Zealand Field Ambulance Hospital. After recovering, Ratan cooked for the New Zealand Reinforcement Camp for three months before being transferred to the 4th Battalion 'A' Company New Zealand Rifle Brigade. He was again hospitalised before a transfer to the 3rd New Zealand Rifle Brigade, 1st Battalion A Company on 20 October 1917. On 3 December that year, he was killed in action at Ypres.[15]

Ratan's name is inscribed on the New Zealand Memorial at Buttes New British Cemetery in Zonnebeke, Belgium. His medals went to his widow, Musammat Lal Devi, of Suten Mandi, Kacha Pir, Bhole, in 1922. By then their only child, Sohan Devi, was aged 21.

keen to serve their new country, two Kiwi-Indian soldiers who bravely fought in Europe during World War I have been publicly remembered: Jagt Singh and Ratan Chand Mehra.

During World War II, most Kiwi-Indians continued to be excluded from military service. Prior to the first conscription ballot for territorial service in October 1940, Circular M.P. 18 was sent to all manpower committees: 'Army Headquarters have instructed Area Officers that if any Indian, Chinaman, Malayan or other Asiatic is called up by ballot, he is not to be medically examined or posted to a unit, and that no action is to be taken with regard to his Military Service.'[16] This advice changed in March 1941, when 'Chinese, Indians and other persons of non-European blood who are British subjects and residents in New Zealand' began to be ordered into camp for territorial service — a shift in policy probably partly due to complaints by European fruiterers that Indian and Chinese competitors had an unfair advantage.[17]

Once industrial conscription for essential industries was brought in during 1942, Indians who were British subjects could be kept in or directed to essential industries. J. O. Liddell, chair of Auckland's Manpower (Industrial) Committee, declared, 'We are not treating these men as Indians, but as British subjects. In wartime they have a liability to do as much for the war effort as other British subjects, European or otherwise.'[18] Some Indians appealed to the manpower committees against these orders because of cultural and religious dietary restrictions or as conscientiously objecting to fight.[19] 'Nana Bhana stated that his religion and beliefs restricted him to a purely vegetarian diet, with special methods of cooking. He was willing to give his services in any capacity which did not interfere with his religious beliefs.'[20]

A circular sent to the members of armed forces appeal boards in March 1941 advised that Asians would not be asked to undertake overseas military service and that all their appeals should be adjourned *sine die*.[21] A few Kiwi-Indians, such as Lachman Singh Mahasha and Munsha Singh Basi, served in the New Zealand armed forces during World War II. Munsha was honoured by the RSA on

Alick and Dudley Mewa: Two different wars

On 19 August 1944, Alick ('Viv' or Vivian) Mewa, a flight lieutenant, with 98 Squadron of the Royal New Zealand Air Force, went missing on a flare-dropping mission over Falaise in France.[22] By then, aged 25, he had completed 57 operational sorties. Alick was the first Indian to gain a commission in the New Zealand Air Force. A year later he was presumed dead.

Alick's father, Ranjan Mewa, had migrated to Aotearoa from Fiji in 1914. He was called up in the draft of May 1918, but by then Indians were not accepted into the New Zealand Expeditionary Force. In 1926 Ranjan's wife, Piyari, and their three sons, Dudley, Alick and Hector, joined him in Auckland. Alick was educated at Richmond Road School and Auckland Grammar School.

In contrast to Alick's wartime sacrifice, his brother Dudley, a civil servant, was detained in a military defaulters' camp during the war. According to news reports, Dudley pleaded '[t]hat he conscientiously objected to service overseas but at the same time considered a slur was being cast on his race through the attitude of the authorities in not accepting Asiatics for military service'.[23] He said that he was a British subject and a Gurkha by nationality. Mr Cox of the Armed Forces Appeals Board pointed out that the authorities were not 'calling on the services of coloured people. This applied mainly to islanders. He had not been aware of appellant's nationality.'

Pilots Alick Mewa (NZ414320) and Mervyn Jack Mills (NZ414321) training in Levin, 1941.

his death at Rotorua during the mid-1960s.[24] Abdul Habib Sahu Khan, an Indo-Fijian medical student studying at Otago University, was awarded a 1939–45 War Medal and New Zealand Service Medal for service during the war.[25] Dr Sahu Khan was later elected as a member of the Fiji Legislative Council from 1957 to 1963.

As in World War I, not all Kiwi-Indian volunteers were accepted for military service. Sixteen-year-old Swaran Singh joined his father Jassa Singh in New Zealand in 1938. In 1940 Swaran tried to join the New Zealand army, but was declined because of inadequate proficiency in the English language. So he left New Zealand and joined the Indian army. After the Japanese surrender he went on to Indonesia with the 5th Indian Division as a scout and was among the first of the invading force in Surabaya.[26]

Although the struggle for India's independence from Britain had reached a peak during World War II, and several Kiwi-Indians resident in India, particularly in Gujarat, were active nationalists, most Indians in New Zealand during World War II supported the war effort. In 1942 at a conference in Taumarunui, the New Zealand Indian Central Association endorsed its support of the New Zealand government's defence policy, offering full cooperation.[27]

Though few saw active service, Indians were essential to New Zealand's war effort in other ways, such as growing vegetables at Pukekohe. Even this was not without controversy, when the Fruit Retailers' Association advocated putting the fruit industry under European control. The Auckland Indian Association stated:

> As far as the war effort is concerned, the Indian Association is most willing to render any service to the Dominion to bring out the war effort at its maximum, and now that the Emergency Regulation Amendment Bill has been passed the Government has every power to call the men on service. If the Government desires that we should be transferred to the productive industries, the Government would manage our business meanwhile. But we really wonder why the Fruit Retailers' Association

> should request that the whole fruit trade should be confined to the European people, which means that we — a small community — would be driven out of the trade. Why should we, if transferred to the productive industries, be put under European supervision and control? [28]

The New Zealand Indian Central Association objected to these proposals, but equally stated its support for both the war effort and India's independence at its annual conference in Taumarunui in 1942:

> The Association wholeheartedly supports the New Zealand Government's defence policy and offers its full co-operation in whatever capacity its services are required. The Association confidently believes that the present war is one of might against right.

A PATRIOTIC HINDU

One of the recent recruits in the Home Guard is a progressive market gardener well-known in the farming community. As a loyal British subject he has thus demonstrated that he is prepared to train and do what he can to equip himself to assist in defending his adopted country. His action shows up in rather sharp contrast the apathy of some eligible New Zealanders who one would expect, with fine British traditions and heroic actions of their forefathers behind them, would have joined up when the first call went out for Guardsmen.

Franklin Times, 9 December 1940

Despite supporting India's attempts to gain independence from Britain, New Zealand's Indian community was also firmly behind the war effort.

The Auckland Indian Association objected to plans to put the market garden industry under European control during the war — effectively driving the Indian community out.

INDIAN FRUITSELLERS.

The Auckland Indian Association, commenting on the Auckland Fruit Retail Traders' Association's statement, has made the following statement:—"As far as the war effort is concerned the Indian Association is most willing to render any service to the Dominion to bring out the war effort at its maximum, and now that the Emergency Regulation Amendment Bill has been passed the Government has every power to call the men on service. If the Government desires that we should be transferred to the productive industries, the Government would manage our business meanwhile. But we really wonder why the Fruit Retailers' Association should request that the whole fruit trade should be confined to the European people, which means that we—a small community—would be driven out of the trade. Why should we, if transferred to the productive industries, be put under European supervision and control?

AUCKLAND INDIAN ASSOCIATION.

Auckland Star, 11 June 1940

The conference is very annoyed at some resolutions passed at the annual meeting of the Europeans' Fruit and Vegetable Association at Auckland. To preach racial discrimination in the twentieth century is to give proof of ignorance and utter lack of present civilisation. In the opinion of the association the best interests of New Zealand will be served by promoting a better understanding of and co-operation in the matter of making New Zealand a Prosperous country.

The Association deems it necessary to point out that India paid its share in the last war and that again she is helping in the present war. The fact should not be overlooked that local Indians being British subjects and also citizens of New Zealand, deserve British justice.

'A splendid note of allegiance'

'A splendid note of allegiance to the British Crown and appreciation of the privileges British citizens enjoy accompanied a gift of £100 received recently by the National Patriotic Fund Board from J. K. Natali, of Waimiha, South Auckland. Mr. Natali is president of the New Zealand Indian Association, but he made it clear in his letter that he made his contribution in his private capacity.

'As an Indian who has settled in this country for the last twenty years who enjoys the benefits of the freedom and liberty under the British Constitution; who is proud of being a British Indian subject; who is conscious of the privileges enjoyed by a full citizenship in this country, and at the same time realising that the privileges also must carry the responsibilities of a citizen.'[29]

— *Evening Post*, 26 January 1940

> The conference notes with regret the attitude adopted by the British government in delaying national freedom to India.[30]

Although many Kiwi-Indians paid taxes, it was not until the 1930s that they were able to claim social welfare benefits from the state. The Old-age Pensions Act, which had been introduced in 1898 as one of the great hallmarks of New Zealand's social welfare state, specifically excluded 'Chinese or other Asiatics, whether

George Calcutta: Denied the old-age pension

G. W. Bates, a resident of Russell, urged the prime minister, Richard Seddon, on 16 March 1904 to make a special case to grant the old-age pension to a British Indian living locally. Known as 'George Calcutta' (although probably from Punjab), he had 'been in the Colony for the last 50 years, working (not hawking or anything of that sort') . . . he has lost all his native habits etc and is thoroughly Europeanised in living and dress etc. He has also practically lost his native language . . . He does not know his age, he does not know the name of the ship he arrived in the Colony in because he was nothing at the time, only an ignorant Indian lad, traveling with his master.'

Bates understood that when George was a child he thought he was going to a distant part of India and that his master, Captain J. C. Johnstone, said he would return George to his home in India. George lived with Johnstone at Raglan until the latter married.[31] He later found work in Auckland, and when he encountered Johnstone again and asked to go home to India, Johnstone 'pooh poohed the matter'. Bates assumed that the people whom George had worked for exploited him 'on account of his friendlessness' (in the sense of being alone) to work for little more than his 'tucker'.[32] During the late 1850s George made his way to the Bay of Islands, where he remained for about 40 years 'working about the district, leading a quiet respectable life and always keeping to himself although very often not treated with the same sense of justice, as regards pay, as his white companions'.

By the time Bates made his plea, George was in his late sixties, doing casual gardening work for two women. Seddon bluntly responded to Bates on 23 March that 'there is no provision for the granting of Old-age Pensions to Asiatics'.[33]

naturalised or not, and whether British subjects or not'. A writer to the minister of pensions suggested on 27 October 1933 that 'no doubt the intention of the legislators . . . was to debar Japanese, Chinese and natives of India from participating in the benefits of the old age pension and thus making this Dominion unattractive as a country of domicile'.[34]

Race (or at least 'Asian race') was the determining factor in granting the old-age pension. The assistant law commissioner ruled on 12 October 1911 that '[i]f an applicant can prove that he has any European blood in his veins, then no matter how largely his Asiatic blood predominates he is not an Asiatic within the meaning' of Section 71 of the Old-age Pensions Act. Thus three Europeans who were born in India were Indian nationals and were granted pensions in 1906 because they had no 'Asian blood'.

Although John Sohman, one of Canterbury's first Indian settlers and a well-respected member of the Oxford community, did secure a pension, the deputy registrar of Kaiapoi informed him on 25 March 1907 that his pension would be cancelled by the registrar of pensions because he (and Austin Nudin, a Malaysian) were 'Asiatics' and, therefore, debarred by clause 64 subsection 4 of the 1898 Pensions Act. This ruling drew condemnation from some correspondents to the media. 'Cosmopolitan' protested

> that the man, who is, I believe, a naturalised New Zealander, is fully entitled to his pension, but that it is being withheld from him through a clause in the Act which precludes Asiatics from sharing in its benefits. Such a clause is iniquitous, and is an instance of that blind racial bigotry so prevalent in this colony. If in the granting or withholding of the pension, any discrimination is to be made, character and not race or colour should be the ground, and the sooner the Act is amended so as to prevent such flagrant injustices as this the better.[35]

An Auckland reception given by the Indian community for Srinivasa Sastri during his visit to New Zealand in 1922. Sastri (centre, front) was an Indian politician sent to Canada, Australia and New Zealand to investigate the living conditions of Indians. To his left are Mrs Cynthia Satwanti Share and Sadanand Maharaj, and to his right are Dr Baldev Singh Share and Mr Hislop (Under Secretary, Internal Affairs). Behind Sastri is Jelal Natali and his wife Kate.

Although the act was amended in 1908, Magistrate Victor Grace Day informed the deputy registrar on 11 November 1908 that he did not have the power to remove Sohman and Nudin's pensions, unless on the ground of proved misconduct or fraud, and their pensions could only be 'taken away by express enactment'. Day doubted whether Section 18 of the 1908 amendment would disqualify some Asiatics unless they came within the description of 'Chinese'.

Yet the commissioner of pensions invoked the fear of an 'Asian invasion' in order to take advantage of New Zealand's social welfare provisions — namely, 'the fear that at any time there might be a considerable influx of population from that Continent who would in due course become eligible under the various other qualifications provided for old age pensions'. He also wanted 'coloured races' from continents outside Asia to be excluded from access to the pension.[36]

Indians were also not entitled to the widows' pension and the family allowance, introduced in 1926, to help maintain children with parents on limited incomes. This act did not apply to 'an Asiatic, whether naturalised or not, or whether a British subject or not'. The First Labour Government repealed social welfare restrictions for Asians under the 1936 Pensions Amendment Act and the 1938 Social Security Act.

State financial and insurance policies also singled out Indians and Chinese. In 1951 Indians were restricted from remitting money to their families in India, ostensibly to discourage them from supporting kin, and to encourage assimilation within New Zealand. In 1957 the Department of Internal Affairs and the Department of External Affairs recommended abolishing this discriminatory practice.

> The fact is that Chinese and Indians are by Reserve Bank instruction not allowed to purchase British postal notes at post offices to any value without Reserve Bank permit. Persons are identified as Chinese or Indian by physical appearance, at least in the first instance. No distinction is made between those who are New Zealand citizens and those who are not. Probably the main reason is the limitation of New Zealand funds remitted to India and China for the support of families. While recognising that this aim is no doubt necessary and desirable, I would suggest that it is not best achieved by discriminating against New Zealand residents, many of them citizens, on grounds of race. I am particularly concerned about the discrimination against one class of New Zealand citizen because he is of Chinese or Indian origin . . . I am inclined to think that it would be more honest and equitable to drop the discrimination based on race and seek the same end by imposing a corresponding restriction on remittance of British postal notes to China and India generally. I realise that this also would be difficult to police, but no more so than the present regulation.[37]

It is not clear when these financial restrictions were amended or abolished.

The ability to remit money to India was not only to support families but also enabled migrants to invest in their own future for when they might retire to their homes in India. But not all of the early Indian settlers in Aotearoa did permanently return, and as we have seen, until 1936, they were excluded from the old-age pension. They also faced difficulties in New Zealand securing another form of cover for old-age — life insurance. The New Zealand Government Life Insurance Department had been established in 1869 to provide affordable policies to workers but for some years policies were not issued to 'full-blooded Maoris,

Chinese, negroes, or other coloured races, but half-castes (excepting Chinese)' were accepted with an extra premium and an early age of maturity.

It is not clear when this policy was amended. As late as the early 1970s Kiwi-Indians were also excluded from taking out life insurance for their children under the New Zealand Government Life Insurance's Children's Deferred Assurance Policy. NZICA raised this with Government Life in 1970, and was informed that 'the Children's Deferred Assurance Policy is not offered to the Indians because of the high mortality rate amongst the Indians'.[38]

six.

Casual and Informal Racism

Over the course of the twentieth century, discrimination against Indians in Aotearoa New Zealand slowly changed at the legislative level. That did not mean an end to racism, which persisted in many guises, often in less institutionalised ways. Covert and casual racism has been one of the most persistently painful challenges to Kiwi-Indians, and one of the most difficult to erase; stereotyping and everyday hostility has impeded many from settling and making a livelihood here.

As early as 1977, American psychologist Chester Pierce and co-researchers coined the term 'racial microaggressions': 'subtle, stunning, often automatic, and non-verbal exchanges which are "put downs"'.[1] Racial microaggressions can be divided into microassaults, microinsults and microinvalidations:

> Microassaults are explicit verbal or non-verbal attacks on an individual that hurt the person and make them feel inferior. Those engaged in their use resort to microassaults when they lose control or there is perceived support for their racist views. Microinsults occur when a person is rude or insensitive when referring to another's racial background or ethnic identity. Finally, microinvalidations are when communications 'exclude,

> negate, or nullify the psychological thoughts, feelings, or experiential reality of a person of color'.[2]

We have already seen how Kiwi-Indians faced informal racism within employment. Casual racism can extend to well-meaning encounters, even friendships, as it is both conscious and hidden, manifested through discourse, jokes or the 'quiet, personal places where racism and prejudice is nurtured'.[3] Waikaremoana Waitoki argues that 'New Zealanders should know that everyday acts of casual racism towards Māori, Pacific, Asians and Muslims is endemic and often silenced'.[4]

The media has been hardly neutral and has been culpable in fomenting both institutional and casual racism: not merely reporting news and anti-Indian discourse, but also framing the way ethnic groups are portrayed.[5] Mainstream media has been and is backed by powerful and wealthy individuals, families and interest groups. As can be seen from the copious examples in this book, the headlines and framing of reports concerning Indians were (and often remain) deliberate, sensational and selective. The most extreme campaign of Indian exclusion was mounted by the *Franklin Times*. The tabloid *NZ Truth* also thrived on stirring up controversy and painted Indians with a racist brush, even when they were the objects of abuse. In 1910, Sali Mahomet, known as 'Ice Cream Charlie', because he sold ice cream in Cathedral Square, Christchurch, was subjected to racial abuse by 17-year-old Robert Meacham. *Truth* reported,

> much as the hooligan is to be deplored, it merely gives articulate expression to the feeling which, in varying

> degrees of refinement, permeates the Caucasian, or transplanted European of all classes . . . still the thought will recur that if the colored gentleman were absent in his own country, the language would not have been used, and it is a matter for regret that Mahomet ever gained admission to this Dominion.[6]

Meacham was fined by the court for the offence. The previous year, *NZ Truth* had published that Sali was 'endangering the White New Zealand movement by keeping a European missus'[7] when the newspaper reported abuse hurled at Sali's wife by a drunken neighbour.

Sali Mahomet, known as 'Ice Cream Charlie', circa 1930, when he worked in Cathedral Square, Christchurch.

The 'luscious lascar'

In 1912, *NZ Truth* opined that Mr Falconer from the Dunedin Seamen's Rest was 'crawling to niggers' when he hosted a Christmas treat of a tour of Dunedin for 21 lascars (Indian seamen) working on a cargo tanker that had berthed at Port Chalmers: 'The party afterwards visited St. Clair, but they did not take part in the bathing. Not much! For two reasons at the very least. Out at St. Clair the young men and young women, who go in for surf bathing, are a clean, healthy, fine physiqued lot, and the young men are strong of arm, and hold stronger views upon a White New Zealand. If Ram Chowdar or Boh Stink had dared to shove his greasy carcase in amongst the surfers, then 'Truth' ventures to say that Ram Chowdar and Boh Stink deceased would have ornamented the sands some days later, and the 'Den of Airlie' would have been two cheap niggers short.

'Second reason is that Lascars don't like water — at any rate for bathing purposes — as it might wash off some of THE 'GHEE' AND PALM OIL from their greasy carcases . . . Dunedin ought to go and HIDE ITS HEAD IN SHAME over this disgraceful episode of the Lascar sailors. The idea of allowing a lot of low-caste Asiatics to mingle with white people is repugnant to everyone but the most ignorant.'[8]

The restrictions Kiwi-Indians faced with immigration and movement across borders was institutional. However, even when entitled to reside within Aotearoa New Zealand or if born there, Kiwi-Indians have been hindered from freedom of movement and residence when hostile individuals or groups have barred Indians from localities and spaces. Such informal discrimination was racial, usually also excluding Māori, Chinese and others not perceived as white. Finding a place to live has been a major hurdle for some Kiwi-Indians.

In 1920 eight Indian scrub-cutters were prevented from living in Masterton. This hostility coincided with an RSA meeting where 'some very straight talk was indulged in against the Hindu menace'. The men moved to Carterton, where they were able to rent a small cottage. This outraged locals: 'Seventy or eighty whites marched up to the cottage and demanded that the Asiatics should move on. They threatened that if they did not do this of their own free will they would be forcibly ejected from the town.'[9] Two police officers arrived and reminded the Indians of their rights and offered protection if they remained in Carterton. But the Indians returned to Masterton, where they had to sleep rough in a park, before dispersing in smaller groups, presumably because this would attract less attention.

Twenty-seven years later, in 1947, New Zealand–born Gulabbhai Moral also encountered discrimination in obtaining accommodation when he was a student at Victoria University:

> I rang on the phone and the wom[a]n answered — and of course I've never had an accent, nobody would recognise that I was an Indian — and she said 'yes there's a vacancy'. So I went along, knocked on the door and as soon as she saw me she said 'I'm sorry it's been taken — there's no vacancy' . . . Well I just didn't say much, and anyhow I got one of my cobbers at university to ring up about three or four hours later and there was still a vacancy there.[10]

Conversely, when Indians did secure a place to live, this might come under public scrutiny. We saw that in Pukekohe 'Hindu shacks' were held up as a warning of the supposed threat to the tidy, neat cottages white families lived in. Before World War II many Indians in Wellington lived in Te Aro, on or near notorious Haining Street, also known as Chinatown.

Kiwi-Indians did not accept derogatory generalisations about their living and working spaces, and made their objections known to media and local bodies. For example, Natali countered the White New Zealand League's depiction of Indian dwellings at Pukekohe, and in 1943 NZICA president Unkabhai Patel hit back about the depictions of Indians' living conditions in the Central North Island.

Racism also erupted when Indians appeared to encroach into intimate spaces reserved for whites. In 1922 Indians in Auckland were refused public access to Auckland City Council's Hobson Street Tepid Baths. One bath was reserved for 'Non-Whites'. Natali wrote to the council on behalf of the Indian community, but restrictions continued.[11]

Since the 1930s Indians also faced exclusion from whites-only spaces in Pukekohe.[12] Barbers refused to cut the hair of Chinese, Māori or Indians. These groups were also banned from the better-quality dress circle within a Pukekohe cinema.

At its annual conference in Christchurch in 1945, the NZICA strongly objected to discrimination against Indians in the theatre at Pukekohe, noting 'the attitude of the theatre owner of Pukekohe towards the Indians who were not allowed to obtain tickets for higher seats were deprecated [*sic*]. The Association believe that it is not only an insult to the Indian Nation but also a disgrace to this country which stands for equality of rights.'[13]

When Lalbhai Patel, a past president of the Auckland Indian Association, raised discrimination against Indians with the Strand Theatre's manager, he was told that Indians were barred because of their untidy dress. Lalbhai pointed out that white potato farmers were allowed to attend daytime sessions on Saturdays in their working clothes. I was informed by a local Indian that the theatre manager told him if Asians were entitled to access the 'privileged' areas of the theatres or barbers' shops, then Māori, too, would have

Slums in the Shadow of Wellington's Carillon

WHERE WELLINGTON PRESENTS AN IRONIC STUDY IN CONTRASTS.

The rooftops of dilapidated dwellings form a sharp contrast to the stately carillon and War Memorial Museum of which Wellington is rightly proud.

New Zealand Observer, 11 February 1937

Illustration from a sensationalist article on Indian and Chinese dwellings in Te Aro, Wellington.

'Get Rid of Haining Street!'

This headline was published in the *New Zealand Observer* in 1937, when 'A.R.M.' described the dwellings on the Te Aro Flat as 'infested with Indians' and also Chinese: 'Now these "shops" are rotting rooms, with windows boarded up. Stored in them by the Indians are fruit and vegetables which are hawked and sold among the homes of Wellington for consumption by men, women and little children. . . . The other two "shops" in this block . . . house the filthy, empty bottles that are collected from all over the city, some direct from householders, some from refuse cans and the like. It is from this evil conglomeration of hawking interests that fruit and vegetables destined for healthy homes set out. . . . I could give you details of the sordid quarters in which Indians live on a wholesale "community" system. I could tell you of the panorama of rusting roofs and filthy yards and of the fetid atmosphere of these crowded junk-heaps. . . . I could tell, too, of the children, yellow, black and white, who play amidst this squalor, but I think I have soiled this page enough.' [14]

INDIAN LIVING CONDITIONS

Sir,—The representative of Indians and the President of The All N.Z. Indian Association (Inc.) Mr Unkabhai K. Patel of Murupara, have given the following comment on the remarks passed by the councillors at a recent meeting of the Whakatane County Council, respecting the conditions of Indians at Murupara, Te Whaiti and Ruatahuna.

The All N.Z. Indian Association resents those remarks as they are untrue and unfair. Those Indians are human, they do not live in hovels, but they have proper houses which are much better than those of most Europeans residing in that district, and also they do not obtain trade by erecting shacks but they have proper up to date authorised stores. By making such general but unfair statements they are insulting Indians and attempting to insinuate that Indians should be looked upon as inferior. The Association believes that those councillors who passed the remarks cannot prove their statements to be true.

Similar descriptions of the living conditions of Kiwi-Indians appeared in other parts of the country. This letter appeared in the *Bay of Plenty Beacon*, 16 November 1943.

to be granted entry.[15] It was not until the 1960s that race restrictions in Pukekohe were eased.[16] For decades, racial hierarchies at Pukekohe were maintained where Pākehā were usually the bosses and Māori the workers, but the presence of a 'third race' — Asians — disturbed this hierarchy through the ambiguity of non-whites as employers and in demands for equal access to public amenities.

Access to purchasing and consuming alcohol has been a powerful demarcation of race in many societies, so it is not that surprising that Kiwi-Indians were sometimes denied entry to bars and hotels. For several decades Indians were excluded from the private bars within Pukekohe hotels. Hotel proprietors in parts of the Waikato also refused to serve liquor to Indians. In 1920 in Te Awamutu, Constable Doyle said that this was because 'Hindus came to town once a week and always got drunk, and went looking for trouble. All through the Waikato this was the same. Farmers and returned soldiers were realising the menace.' He claimed, too, 'Hindus were becoming a menace to women and children in the district.' Doyle's testimony followed a brawl between drunk 'Hindu farmers and Europeans'.[17] Although both groups were convicted of offences, the media planted the blame on the Indians. (Note again that Indians were called Hindus, although the majority of Indians working in the King Country were Sikhs.)

Over 30 years later, at a hotel in Christchurch in 1952, Indians were again barred from consuming alcohol. The rationale was simply racist; there was no threat to law and order, and the clients were well-dressed delegates at NZICA's annual conference. NZICA complained to the hotel manager, Christchurch's mayor and the Canterbury Licensed Victuallers' Association.[18]

NZICA had also objected in 1945 when Indians were singled out

'No European Need Apply'

This condition was made as an unusual form of protest about housing discrimination against non-whites in 1949 when a retired church worker advertised a house with two flats for sale in Dominion Road, Auckland. The house was for sale only to Chinese, Hindu, Māori and other 'coloured' people. The advertisement read: 'Even in New Zealand she has known of decent coloured people discriminated against, and insults heaped on them. She feels that she can do something for at least one family.'[19]

as the culprits for violating prohibitions imposed on Māori access to alcohol within 'dry' zones such as the King Country. The police commissioner alleged that Indians sold liquor to Māori on marae, and also to Māori elsewhere, including Auckland, and so Indians should be prohibited from taking alcohol home from hotels. NCICA President Jalal Natali objected to this discriminatory suggestion in a submission he made to the Royal Licensing Commission. He acknowledged that some Indians had been convicted of supplying liquor to Māori, but the commission's evidence showed that most illicit liquor was supplied by Europeans. In Natali's words:

> There was more drunkenness and sly-grogging among Europeans than among Indians . . . we are also very sensitive people and resentful to any discriminating laws against us . . . we will not agree to any laws that will lower our status.[20]

Hasmukh Dullabh selling newspapers outside a bottle store in Vivian Street, Wellington, circa 1959–60.

Motiram Vallabh: Refused to vacate his seat at the Strand Theatre

Times were tough during the Great Depression for Bhagabhai Vallabh and his two sons, Motiram and Naran. They leased small plots of land around Pukekohe where they grew potatoes. At the worst of times they were unable to sell or give away their crops. A landowner, Mr Pellow, deferred rental payments so that Bhagabhai could obtain credit to buy seed, sprays and fertiliser for the following season.[21] Bhagabhai was used to hard work: he had emigrated to New Zealand in 1918 from Sisodra-Alak in Gujarat and then worked on dairy farms in the Hauraki Plains before hawking fruit and vegetables, and collecting bottles in Auckland. His sons joined him after he settled in Pukekohe in 1926.

Like many young Kiwis of his era, Motiram occasionally escaped from economic hardship to watch the movies – for him the option was an evening at Pukekohe's Strand Theatre. On 4 March 1933 at 7.30 p.m. he tried to pay two shillings for a seat in the dress circle to see the movie *Mr George Arliss*. The ticket box attendant informed Motiram that there were no seats upstairs – ostensibly because these seats were booked out; this being a popular night for movie goers, after the horse races had finished. Motiram bought a ticket to the general area and sat on a seat where there was no reserved sign.

The movie programme started – probably with the short item *Naggers at the Dentist*, billed as 'a matrimonial comedy' – but Motiram was asked to vacate the seat by proprietor Brian Blennerhassett, who claimed that it was reserved. When Motiram refused, Blennerhassett attempted to physically remove him. Motiram would not budge, and the proprietor asked a fireman and a police officer to eject Motiram from his seat. He temporarily left during the programme's interval, but was denied readmission. So Motiram engaged the services of a lawyer, E. G. Foster, and claimed the refund of his admission money and £25 damages because he had been assaulted.

Motiram revealed to the court that on three previous occasions, he had experienced trouble over reserved seats, even when there were very few people in the theatre. Twice he had sat down on a seat, but was shifted to the front. Motiram always objected to this and his money was refunded. But on a third occasion he and his uncle were simply refused efforts to reserve seats upstairs in the dress circle.

The magistrate ruled in favour of Motiram because after purchasing a ticket he was legally entitled to enter the cinema, occupy any one-shilling seat which was not reserved, and view the programme. Motiram was awarded £10 in damages, a 1s entrance charge and costs of £5 9s.

In 1943, Bhagabhai Vallabh purchased a property in Upper Queen Street. Four years later he retired to his village in Gujarat.[22]

Motiram Vallabh (left), Naran Parbhu and Naran Vallabh relaxing after work at Vallabh's on Queen Street, Auckland, during the late 1950s.

In 1922, Indians were refused access to Auckland's Tepid Baths. These letters to the editor from the *Auckland Star* express outrage at the racist and exclusionary practice.

CITY COUNCIL'S BATHS.

(To the Editor.)

Sir,—I quite agree with "Fond of Baths" about the discrimination shown towards the dark-skinned British subjects in Hobson Street Baths. I and my other countrymen received the same treatment from the bath authorities. On behalf of my countrymen I appealed to the City Council, but the reply from the council did not give us any satisfaction. This matter was put before the City Council's meeting held on July 27, but our claim as Empire citizens for equality of treatment received scant consideration.—I am, etc.,

JELAL KALYANJI NATALI.

Auckland Star, 22 July 1922

A CASE OF DISCRIMINATION.

(To the Editor.)

Sir,—I would like to draw attention to the difference in treatment between white and dark skinned people at the tepid baths. I, who am a dark skinned British subject, have been using the bath rooms for many months. To-day on essaying to enter one of the rooms the attendant stopped me, and said I could not use it, as all, except one bath, were reserved for white people. As that one was engaged I handed in my towel and left the baths. I consider that the people of our nation are quite as clean in every way as any white people, and do not deserve such humiliating treatment. Also if the baths are properly cleansed after each bather, what difference does it make who used them previously?—I am, etc.,

FOND OF BATHS.

Auckland Star, 17 July 1922

Many Indian pioneers and their descendants have been the brunt of stereotypes. These might reflect ignorance by other New Zealanders who considered their offhand remarks part of the Kiwi way of 'leg-pulling'. But cruel remarks that denigrated Indian identity could impose lifelong individual and collective hurt, even if Kiwi-Indians did not openly object to the stereotypes and insults, or even seemed to play along with the joke. Angelique Nairn explains how

> microaggressions can be confused, dismissed or considered innocuous by those using them because they can be communicated unconsciously and unintentionally . . . [and] that those on the receiving end of racial microaggressions often granted individuals the benefit of the doubt because intent could not be readily discerned . . . receivers may excuse discriminatory microaggressions, despite their cumulative effect being considered more severe than overt racism.[23]

Although during the early twentieth century Wallabh Soma Moral was respected in New Plymouth, along with his family and friends he experienced a 'hard time from the locals about being Indians'. His well-patronised shop was known as 'Nigger's Corner', possibly also because Māori congregated nearby.[24] This points to the common discrimination levelled at Māori and Indians.

Another example of casual racism was the changing of names at birth, when hospital staff suggested or unilaterally recorded European names on birth certificates. Thus 'Arun' might become 'Alan', Jagdish was called Jack, Nagin became Neil and Premila was Pam.

School was another place where Kiwi-Indian children might find their name changed, sometimes to their surprise and without their consent. Mandrika Rupa recalled when she started at Blockhouse Bay Primary in 1960:

> I got the shock of my life when I first enrolled because coming from Newton, [with] what was a big ethnic

English names were often imposed on Kiwi-Indians. From left: Ganda Singh ('Jim'), Kehar Singh ('Kaira'), Varyam Singh ('Vram'), Daya Kaur ('Nellie') holding Tej Kaur ('Annie'), circa 1914, South Westland.

> majority there, and I remember my first day at primary school, the headmaster, Mr Abbott, took me to the class I was going to be in and he said my name and the teacher, Miss Brown, immediately said oh we couldn't possibly say that name, she has to be called Mandy so there you are, that was the starting of my new identity, I had to conform. I think I just was confused, I just thought what's that, I wonder what that means and then you still think, oh well that's not a bad name, that's fine, okay I can deal with that — I just felt it was difficult to participate because your viewpoint was not represented.[25]

Immigrants might be intentionally given new names by customs officers; equally, Indian immigrants chose to change their names upon arrival in New Zealand, to facilitate immigration clearance and avoid future stereotypes in the new country. Esup Musa took the name Joseph Moses when he arrived around 1910 at Auckland.[26] Abdullah Shada, originally from Lahore, worked as a hawker for several years in Rangitīkei District under the name of Simon George, which he used when he applied for naturalisation as a New Zealand citizen in 1903.

Workmates and neighbours often imposed English names upon Indians. This was possibly because they could not be bothered to pronounce exotic sounds, or it may have been a genuine effort to include newcomers into local communities. Ganda Singh acquired the name of Jim, and his wife, Daya Kaur, that of Nellie, in the mining camps of early twentieth-century Westland.[27] Jelal Natali's workmates called him Mick because he sounded like a 'bloody Irishman' demanding Home Rule from the British when he went on about independence for India.

Naming has also, however, been blatantly derogatory and ridden with stereotypes. Rafik Patel, son of Yakub Mohammed Patel of Bharuch, Gujarat and Julica Ebrahim (Mussa) Patel of Tauranga, was born in Aotearoa in 1974. He recalls growing up in Auckland 'during a period where the racial slur "Curry Muncher"

Shantiben Bava: Given a European name at birth

Maniben Bava was the first Indian woman to settle in Pukekohe in 1936. The following year, she and her husband Dhanabhai were the proud parents of probably the first Gujarati girl born in the Auckland region at Burwood Hospital. Burwood's matron was anxious the birth was correctly registered, so chose Margaret, after the name of a hospital employee. Margaret was later given her Indian name Shantiben by her parents. This naming pattern followed for six other Bava children born before 1952: John, Jean, Ronald, Pamela, Janet, Colin and Ross — who were, respectively, Nanabhai, Kamalaben, Jivanbhai, Premilaben, Nandiben, Naranbhai and Govindbhai.[28]

Dhanabhai Bava with Nanabhai, and Maniben Bava with Kamalaben. Standing is Shantiben, circa 1940.

was commonly used to stereotype Indians aggressively'.[29]

Racial stereotypes were also perpetuated from self-styled experts on Indian culture. In the 1920s, 'Pandion', a retired judge who lived in India, projected stereotypes about 'Our Asiatics' for the *Franklin Times* that were lapped up by many New Zealanders.[30] Pandion said Indians in New Zealand were vastly inferior representatives of their culture and typified the lowest and most degraded kinds of Asians. He argued that since Indians had left India and presumably broken caste rules, they were subsequently free from any moral restraint:

> The Indians cannot escape the feeling that in a like amalgamation they are breaking the most sacred of their social traditions of their motherland. Now, when men consciously break social tradition they are apt to become loud and aggressive. And this is what is actually happening. The Chinese are quietly and unassumingly keeping to themselves and building up fortunes with which they look forward to retiring in comfort eventually in China. The Indians, on the other hand, swagger about earning when they feel like it, loafing when they don't, but in any case spending when they do earn . . . They are compelled by circumstance to offend against every caste every day, and what hope have they of a welcome in India if they should return there from this Dominion.[31]

Pandion's 'first hand knowledge' was wrong. Indians in New Zealand were, when he wrote, mostly Gujaratis and Punjabis. They had hardly violated social traditions in leaving India, as the very act of migration was a means by which to enhance social status. Emigration had been established for hundreds of years in the home villages from which Kiwi-Indians originated. Very few Indian migrants were lazy or recklessly spent money, either. Most worked extremely hard, usually lived frugally and scrupulously saved their earnings. The goal of retirement in their birthplace was not confined to Chinese migrants, as Pandion claimed, but was also important to many Kiwi-Indians (as Bhagabhai Vallabh's story shows). Pandion also was unaware that many Indian migrants in New Zealand had a relatively high status and important role to play in their home villages in India.

But Pandion's racial slurs were endorsed by the editor of the *Franklin Times,* who asserted that the Indian migrant was a 'pariah' and an 'outcast',[32] and that the Indians who had settled at Pukekohe were not the 'true' Aryans of India, but, rather, the majority of the 'Hindoos we have are Bengalese, a cowardly race'. The following year the editor took the opportunity to compare the 'Aryan' Indian hockey team with the local Indians:

> Unfortunately, we in New Zealand know but little of the Aryans of India. A few of them come here and work for a while, but they do not settle in this country. Our knowledge of India is practically confined to inhabitants of Central India, a degraded race that would be exterminated tomorrow by the war-like Northerners, who detest and despise them, were the sovereignty of the British raj removed.[33]

Bureaucratic discourse, while not enshrined in legislation, could be just as nasty as the words splashed across newspapers or in children's playground taunts. Some bureaucrats (those former colonial officers who had 'real' Indian experience) also claimed expertise about specific races. In 1955 the secretary of labour wrote to Bill Sullivan, minister of immigration, that Indians have a 'reputation of being the world's most untruthful people and departmental experience fully confirms this'.[34] Although there were only 2425 Indians in New Zealand at the 1951 census, the

Mary (Meri) Ahipene-Hoete and Nagar Hari, photographed on 4 January 1969 at the wedding of Luxmme and Peter Underwood, at the Methodist Church, Taumarunui.

secretary warned that the growth of the Indian population over the previous 35 years indicated that, unless the firmest possible steps were taken, the situation could get out of hand.

A senior government official during the 1960s stated that the Gujaratis in New Zealand were not 'caste Hindus' because they collected bottles and some were employed in ritually demeaning work such as street-cleaning and shoemaking.[35] Such cultural ignorance was blind not only to the realities of Indian migrants finding any work in New Zealand, but also to the fact that most Kiwi-Gujaratis had a *jat* or caste (even those working in manual work). And in any case, by 1961 very few Gujaratis in Aotearoa were bottle collectors, street cleaners or shoemakers. Revel Lochore, High Commissioner for New Zealand in New Delhi, admitted that his knowledge of Gujaratis was inadequate, but curiously deemed them 'New Zealand's least successful immigrant community'[36] — at odds with Indians' growing reputation as a 'model minority' in Aotearoa.

We have traced how Indians were excluded at different levels in New Zealand and how casual racism was pervasive in many guises. Yet some Pākehā,[37] and more notably Māori, went far beyond merely tolerating an Indian presence, and extended friendship and manaakitanga (hospitality) towards Indians. During the early twentieth century, close and intimate relationships developed between Māori and Indian hawkers, such as Jaga Rupa, Kala Rupa and Tainui in the Waikato.[38] Two of Jagabhai's sons settled at Aramiro and married Māori women. Santa Singh, as noted earlier, made the long journey up into te Urewera to deliver goods to Rua Kēnana, the Tūhoe prophet. Patu, one of Rua's daughters, and Sheru Ram would establish a family in Whakatāne.[39] Not only did Indian

'Maori boys and an Indian boy walking down the road,' Waikato, 1938. Photograph by Leo White.

Newspaper articles showing moral panic over Māori women and Indian men living together.

INDIANS AND MAORIS

UNDESIRABLE INTIMACY.

(BY TELEGRAPH.—PRESS ASSOCIATION.)

HAMILTON, This Day.

The undesirable intimacy which is springing up between Indians who are overrunning the King Country and Natives in different localities was brought under the notice of the Waikato Hospital Board in a special report from Nurse Moore, of Manunui, who complains that illicit relationship between the two races is becoming a serious menace to the morals of the Maoris. Indians appear to have got into the confidence of the Maori women, and there have recently been two births to Indian fathers.

Evening Post, 11 April 1914

ASIATICS AND MAORIS.

PROBLEM TO BE DISCUSSED.

The Maniapoto District Maori Council will discuss the effects of young Maori women living with Indians in the vicinity of Te Kuiti and Otorohanga, at a conference to be held at Te Kuiti to-morrow.

It is possible that the Auckland native organisation, Te Akarana Maori Association, will have a representative at the conference. The association has been instrumental in showing the results of the mingling of Maoris and Asiatics, and it intends to co-operate with the Maniapoto Council.

Members of the Akarana Association were given by Mr. T. Hotu definite instances of the degradation of Maori women associated with Indians. Mr. Hotu stated that Waikato Maoris were anxious to remove the Asiatic influence.

New Zealand Herald, 7 August 1929

men form relationships with Māori women, but in later years some Indian women, such as Maniben Unka and her daughters in Rotorua during the 1950s, had warm friendships with Māori neighbours, especially through cooking and eating together.[40]

Indian–Māori relationships, no matter how loving, mutually respectful or caring, evoked the ire of both Māori and Pākehā. This came to prominence with the investigation into the employment of Māori, and particularly women, by Chinese and Indians on market gardens in 1929. There were fears of the Māori 'full-blooded race' being diluted and degraded through, as Andrew Ngawaka of Te Akarana Maori Association put it in 1929, Māori women living with Hindus and Chinese.[41] The Akarana Maori Association pushed for legislation to prevent future 'alliances' between Indians and Māori. The Maori Methodist Synod passed a resolution requesting government to introduce a bill to prevent intermarriage between Hindus and Māori, although there were fewer objections to Māori marrying into the 'British race'.[42]

The number of mixed births of Asian and Māori or European parentage was indeed increasing in New Zealand, but hardly at a rate indicative of the formation of a 'hybrid race'.[43] In 1936 the census recorded 292 people of 'mixed-blood' (mostly Indian-European) and 41 of Indian-Māori descent. It is possible that the latter number was higher, as those with Indian and Māori parentage may have been enumerated under the separate Māori census. Indeed, at Pukekohe, the centre of such panic, only one Indian of mixed descent was recorded at the 1926 and 1936 censuses.[44] But in 1934 Sir Āpirana Ngata still argued that 'we do not want Maori slaves wandering about New Zealand mating with the Chinese and the Hindus — people who are alright in their own country, but, in white New Zealand and white Australia, are undesirable'.[45] So white New Zealand could encompass Māori, but not Indians.[46]

At the 2018 census, 4806 people in Aotearoa identified as Māori Indian.

seven.

Contemporary Exclusion

Aotearoa New Zealand would seem to have become kinder and more inclusive towards Kiwi-Indians by the late twentieth century. Immigration policy became somewhat more liberal towards Indians after 1974, and especially after the 1987 Immigration Act. From then the Kiwi-Indian population grew substantially and diversified in terms of national origins, cultures, religion, gender and class. At the 2018 census, about 231,099 individuals or 4.7 per cent of Aotearoa's population identified their ethnicity as Indian, an increase from 155,000 in 2013. As at 2018, 111,348 Indians in New Zealand were born in India, reflecting both recent immigrants and the established communities of Kiwi-Indians, many of whom were born in Gujarat and Punjab but had lived most of their lives in Aotearoa.

Kiwis of South Asian heritage have far greater visibility within a wider range of occupations and locations than 100 years ago. Sukhi Turner (Dame Sukhinder Kaur Gill Turner), who was born in Ludhiana, Punjab, and emigrated to New Zealand in 1973, served as the mayor of Dunedin from 1995 until 2004. Ashraf Choudhary, an environmental scientist and agricultural engineer, was Aotearoa's first parliamentarian (with the Labour Party) from South Asia. Originally from the Punjab region of Pakistan, and the nation's first Muslim member of Parliament, he served from 2002 to 2011. Winston Peters, then leader of the New Zealand First party, said it was a breach of proper procedure when Choudhary was sworn in as a member of Parliament on the Qur'an.

Sir Anand Satyanand was governor-general from 2006 to 2011, and the first of Indian descent in this role. Kanwaljit Singh Bakshi, who emigrated to Aotearoa in 2001, represented the National Party from 2008 to 2020 and was New Zealand's first Indian and Sikh member of Parliament. The 2020 parliamentary elections ushered in four members of Parliament of South Asian descent, all with the Labour Party. Priyanca Radhakrishnan, born in Chennai and from Singapore, is serving her second term in Parliament. She was the first cabinet minister of Indian ethnicity when she was appointed minister for the community and voluntary sector, diversity, inclusion and ethnic communities and youth. Dr Gaurav Sharma, originally from Himachal Pradesh, took his 2020 parliamentary oath in Sanskrit and te reo Māori.[1] Invercargill-born Dr Ayesha Verrall's mother was originally from the Maldives. As an infectious diseases physician and researcher, Verrall was a prominent expert during New Zealand's Covid-19 response in 2020. She is currently minister for seniors, minister for food safety, associate minister of health and associate minister for research, science and innovation. Vanushi Walters was born in Sri Lanka and was a lawyer before being elected to Parliament in 2020.

Food and sports appear to be visible signs of the acceptance of Indian cultures within Kiwi culture. Sports came first; Kiwi-Indians have long been enthusiastic and successful sports players and followers, especially of cricket and hockey.[2] Indian cuisine is now embraced by many Kiwis, and Indian festivals, notably Diwali, are publicly celebrated throughout the country.[3] Indian media and music is widely available, and since 2002 there has even been a

Swaroopa Prameela Unni performing Bharatanatyam in collaboration with Taonga Pouro artists Jessie Jack and Shannon Van Rooijen at Kavanagh College Auditorium, Dunedin, in 2016. Swaroopa migrated to Ōtepoti Dunedin in 2010 from Kozhikode (Calicut) in Kerala and founded the Natyaloka School of Indian Dance. This performance is *Yathra — The Journey*, which showed the journey of migrants who settled in Ōtepoti.

Miss India New Zealand pageant. Today there are several striking Indian religious and community buildings throughout the country's main centres.[4] By 2011 the Asia New Zealand Foundation reported a marked increase (to 55 per cent) in positivity towards Asian people in New Zealand.[5]

New Zealand's 1993 Human Rights Act offers legislative protection against discrimination on the basis of ethnicity, race or nationality. The act consolidated the 1971 Race Relations Act and the 1977 Human Rights Commission Act. Section 61 of the 1993 act prohibits the exciting of hostility and bringing groups of people into contempt.[6] The act established a Human Rights Commission, to which Kiwi-Indians can lodge complaints about discrimination. The commission may follow up with mediation or refer complaints to the Human Rights Review Tribunal.

But have these changes led to more acceptance of Kiwi-Indians and less discrimination? Although it may appear that Aotearoa is more inclusive, evidence indicates that 'we are not one' and reveals an appalling record of not only discrimination towards Kiwi-Indians but also the scars of physical violence. It could be argued that such aggression is because some Kiwi-Indians work in vulnerable occupations, but this hardly exonerates the litany of verbal abuse at the street level, from some politicians, and in the media.

Other factors have contributed towards an upsurge during the twenty-first century of exclusionary discourse and hostile actions towards Kiwi-Indians. Islamophobia has heightened globally and locally since the terrorist attacks in the US of 11 September 2001 ('9/11'), the 2002 Bali bombings and the London attacks in 2005.[7] Since these atrocities, Kiwi-Muslim women, many of Indian and Pakistani origin, have been verbally abused when wearing

'No Indians': Rotorua Christchurch flat ads 'racist'

WELLINGTON BAR LABELS INDIAN PATRONS AS RAPISTS

Racial attack: Kiwi beaten, verbally abused in daylight assault in Auckland's Sandringham

Girl suffers racial abuse at Dunedin park

'Go back to your country' — Kiwis share racism stories

KIWI-INDIAN SIKH SUBJECTED TO RACIST SLUR IN SOUTH AUCKLAND- 'GO BACK TO YOUR COUNTRY'

Wellington train conductor stops and demands a racist passenger to get off

Racism claims sour soccer club's victory

Foxton chef peppered by racist spray

INDIAN TENANTS DENIED RENTAL PROPERTY BECAUSE 'INDIANS ARE DIRTY'

Racism blamed for bar ban

Migrant nurses in New Zealand face racism daily

Indian migrants face job discrimination: study

PARTNERSHIP VISA: IT'S TIME TO CLEAR DIRT AROUND KIWI-INDIAN COMMUNITY

Shane Jones says Indian students have 'ruined' NZ academic institutions

A sample of contemporary media headlines.

From top: *Otago Daily Times*, 20 September 2019; *Indian Weekender*, 13 January 2014; *New Zealand Herald*, 5 June 2019; *Otago Daily Times*, 15 January 2020; *New Zealand Herald*, 17 June 2018; *Indian Weekender*, 27 February 2017; *New Zealand Herald*, 10 August 2019; *Hawke's Bay Today*, 3 September 2012; *Horowhenua Chronicle*, 7 August 2019; *Indian Weekender*, 16 May 2019; *New Zealand Herald*, 3 January 2014; *New Zealand Herald*, 19 July 2018; *Otago Daily Times*, 24 November 2011; *Indian Weekender*, 7 November 2019; *Newshub*, 29 February 2020.

distinctive dress, such as the hijab.[8] Mosques have been desecrated, such as when Philip Neville Arps dumped a box of pigs' heads at Christchurch's Masjid Al-Noor in March 2016.

It is easy to blame anti-Indian behaviour on the growth of neo-Nazi and alt-right groups, globally and within Aotearoa. Many alt-right groups comprise young men who see themselves as disenfranchised and use social media to foment race hatred through, for instance, predictions that the white race will become extinct because of non-white immigration. In March 2017, a new club calling itself the Auckland University European Students Association distributed white supremacist posters on the University of Auckland campus during orientation week. Amid the resulting furore, the club disbanded, but a week later Winston Peters visited Victoria University of Wellington and publicly reprimanded the media for suppressing free speech. This drew praise from white supremacists in New Zealand, one of whom demanded, 'I want someone to get rid of the Indians and Chinese, those f****** are stealing our country right out from under us.'[9]

The terrorist responsible for the 15 March 2019 massacre in Christchurch was consumed by such discourse. But, as this book has shown, the roots of prejudice against South Asians, and other non-white migrants pre-date the rise of social media. In 1997 in the Bishopdale Mall in Christchurch, a woman of Pakistani descent had her hijab torn off by three skinheads, who also ran away with her baby. The following day a group of young men surrounded and abused a Nigerian immigrant and his family when they were relaxing on Sumner beach in Christchurch. He was attacked when he ran for police help. It seems that there were hundreds of people witnessing the assault, but only two intervened.[10]

It was during the early 1990s that talk of 'influx' and 'invasion' became common from politicians and within the media, notably through material such as the 'inv-Asian' articles by Pat Booth and Yvonne Martin, published by the *Eastern Courier* in 1993, and Deborah Coddington's cover story for *North & South* in December 2006, which asked, 'Asian angst. Is it time to send

'Who are the New Zealanders?'[11]

Karuna Muthu and his wife and daughter migrated to Aotearoa in 1995 from Tamil Nadu and took citizenship in 1999. In September 2002 he led a small protest to the steps of Parliament, where he shouted 'stop racism' at Winston Peters, leader of the New Zealand First party.

During the previous month Peters had given an inflammatory speech in Parliament, claiming that the minister of immigration had allowed 'necrophiliacs, triple murderers, killers, rapists, fraudsters' into the country.[12] Muthu had requested the Speaker of the House of Representatives, Jonathan Hunt, expunge Peters' remarks from the parliamentary record, while Peters denied that he had even said these things. Muthu protested against Peters 'tarring all migrants with the same brush' and 'instigating xenophobia and racism'. He added that 'what hurts most of all . . . is Mr Peters's implication that migrants are not New Zealanders, that they have no commitment to the country, and therefore do not count as true citizens'.

Peters refused to answer reporters' questions as to whether he considered immigrants to be New Zealanders. In a speech on 28 August 2002, Peters described Prime Minister Helen Clark's electoral campaign headquarters on election night as like the United Nations. 'One could not find a New Zealander there; everybody but a New Zealander was there.'[13] Muthu asked, 'Who are the New Zealanders? Doesn't he accept me as a New Zealander? What does it mean? I will leave it up to the general public whether that is racism or not.'[14]

some back?' Although these articles did not target Indians, they helped fuel a moral panic about Asian immigration.[15] Kiwi-Indians became subsumed within stereotypes of Asian immigrants, and research that measured New Zealanders' perceptions of Asians indicated a strong negative response at that time.[16] By 2010 the

Human Rights Commission disclosed that Asian people reported higher levels of discrimination than any other minority in New Zealand, while the United Nations Committee on the Elimination of Racial Discrimination highlighted New Zealand's 'persistent discrimination against migrants, particularly of Asian origin'.[17]

Since the 1990s, Kiwi-Indians operating shops, such as dairies, superettes and liquor stores, have been vulnerable to violent attacks. Some may argue that such attacks were more likely because of where these businesses were located and their long hours of operation. But as Paul Patel told TV3 on 26 January 2008, many Indian shopkeepers were 'always on edge' and felt helpless. In October 1993, Navin Govind was brutally murdered and his 10-year-old son Sanjay Govind assaulted in the family superette in Auckland.[18] On 29 August 2000, Indo-Fijian Shiu Prasad, a liquor store owner in Māngere, was murdered for takings of $220 by a man who had previously been charged with three other aggravated robberies of Indian-owned businesses in the area.[19] On 19 June 2005, shop worker Bhagubhai Vaghela was fatally shot in Uptown Minimart in Auckland. Krishna Naidu, a 22-year-old tertiary student, was working in his family's store in Clendon when he was stabbed to death by a 16-year-old on 25 January 2008.[20] A family friend, Giyannendra Prasad, explained how the Naidu family had come to Aotearoa from Fiji in 2001 to build a new future for themselves after George Speight's coup. 'One senseless, mindless, cruel, callous, kindless act robbed Krishna from that forever. Krishna's life has been taken away in a country they'd accepted as their new home.'[21] As recently as August 2020, Mohammed Khan's mini market in Palmerston North was stormed by three masked men wielding a

Sushila Budhia: Woman alone

In 1970, an arranged marriage brought 18-year-old Sushila from Bombay to Christchurch to marry Hira Makan Budhia. Coming from what she depicted as a liberal family, she had to adjust as the new bride within her husband's somewhat more traditional Gujarati family, which was by then three generations. In 1979 the young couple branched out, 'mortgaging themselves to the eyeballs to buy a corner dairy' — Avenue Dairy on the corner of Christchurch's Worcester Street and Fitzgerald Avenue.

After Hirabhai passed away on 31 July 1981, aged only 32, Sushila (known as Sue) operated the dairy, raised their two young daughters, Alpa and Sangeeta, and built up her property investments. In 1983, she faced the first of many potentially violent attempts to rob the dairy. She became resolute at fending off these attacks, sometimes with a hockey stick, including one occasion when six assailants were armed with guns and knives. Sushila also did not tolerate racist abuse: 'You're telling this black bitch to go back home are you, dear? Well, if this black bitch goes back to Bombay who will pay the taxes that put the bread in your mouth?'

Dairies have long served as community hubs in urban and rural Aotearoa. Sushila was lauded by journalist Cate Brett as the 'de facto sheriff of inner-city east Christchurch and her corner dairy its de facto community centre'. Sinead O'Hanlon described Sushila as 'the area's unofficial mother, agony aunt, social worker, and philosopher. Other people faced with the threats of violence she has faced might barricade themselves behind locked doors. Instead, Mrs Budhia does all she can to help the disadvantaged of her area. As a result, her shop is constantly busy with customers who come to buy and others who just come to talk.'[22]

Navin Govind: 'Attacks like this make us all victims'

In a moving and graphic article published in *Metro* in 1994, journalist Nicola Legat stressed that the senseless murder of Navin Govind in 1993 took place in a dairy, as good as a public place.[23] Dairies have been very much part of Kiwi history and culture,[24] where Indians were prominent. While Legat does not explicitly pin the blame for this tragedy on racism against Indians, she speaks to how Navin's murder makes victims of all of us — including the three young assailants.

Navin came to Aotearoa from Gujarat at the age of 10 to join his father, who worked as a labourer with New Zealand Rail. His mother was a labourer with Donaghy's Ropes. Navin attended Mount Albert Grammar and then trained as a fitter and turner. In 1974 he married 19-year-old Joshna, also from Gujarat, and she joined Navin to live with his parents in Mount Albert. Their first child, Ceilla, was born in 1975. The restructuring of public services in New Zealand during the early 1980s brought many redundancies and Navin was not exempt. In 1985 he and Joshna bought a Four Square shop in Kelston, which they named Navin and Joshna's. Ceilla later recalled, 'The point to it, like for many parents, was the children . . . That was their aim — to get me to university. That's what they wanted for me and that's what I wanted too.'[25] Joshna told Legat: 'We worked 12 hours a day, from eight to eight, but there was always time for the children. Every evening when we all came home we would go into the living room and sit and talk for half an hour, maybe an hour, that was the rule . . . Every Saturday was our day for the family. We didn't have visitors. We didn't go out anywhere. Someone wanted to watch the league on TV, then we all watched it together. If someone wanted to watch something else, then we all watched that.' Sadly Joshna died in 2006 at the age of 50.

Navin and Joshna Govind photographed in their home in Auckland, 1992.

'Racial Abuse Rife Says Taxi Driver'

In the past there was opposition when a few Indians began to drive taxis. But the extent of physical and verbal abuse against Indian taxi-drivers appears to have burgeoned in contemporary Aotearoa. The *Herald on Sunday* noted, for instance, how 'Tauranga Mount Taxis driver, Gurmeet Singh, was viciously bashed in January 2013. He saw the attack as racially motivated and told media that "Race-based abuse is a fact of life in the taxi industry".'[26] Other Kiwi-Indian drivers in Tauranga had lost teeth and had their turbans ripped off them. Singh remained fearful long after the attack and subsequently only occasionally drove his taxi. Jacqui Coffey, a spokesperson for Tauranga Mount Taxis, reported, "I get people saying,' Can I have a white driver'? I say, 'Actually no, you can't request that' . . . I've had people ring up saying, 'Do you have to send me a towel head'?"'

knife, screwdriver and hammer — one of three shop robberies within two weeks in the city.[27]

Violence against Indians in Aotearoa did not just take place in shops. In 1991 Indian guest-workers who had been hired to pick squash in Hawke's Bay had gunshots fired at their caravans. Indian workers in Hastings were again the target of a home invasion in 2000 that left three hospitalised after beatings with a baseball bat; one victim lost an eye. This was the fifth local attack on immigrants reported to police in seven weeks, which led Detective Senior Sergeant Mike Wilkinson to suggest that 'the increase in the number of crimes involving or directed at immigrants might also be because more immigrants were living in Hastings than ever before'.[28]

Other South Asians who have suffered violence were hardly within so-called vulnerable occupations or spaces. In 1994, graffiti reading 'White Power' was sprayed on the house of an Indian family that had migrated from South Africa to Hamilton. During this period the swastika defaced the homes and businesses of other South Asians in Hamilton.[29] Late one Monday night in November 1997 an explosive device was thrown at the door of an Indian family's home in Havelock North, not only causing damage inside the house but also terrifying an 'elderly' woman, who had to be treated for shock.[30] In 2010 a 71-year-old Indian man had his turban knocked off and his false teeth punched out by a young man in Hastings. While being sentenced to two years and three months' imprisonment, the assailant kept using racist terms and showed no remorse. The judge summed it up as a 'disgraceful race-based attack. Not the kind we're used to in New Zealand and we certainly don't tolerate that kind of behaviour.'[31] The *Spinoff* reported that on Queen's Birthday Weekend in June 2019, just three months after the Christchurch mosque attacks, a man who had emigrated from India two years before was

> enjoying the June winter sunshine, walking the deserted midday streets of Sandringham. As he crossed Fowlds Ave a silver hatchback surged towards him; its crew of young men leered. The man ran across the avenue and down a footpath; the car's engine followed. He heard doors slamming, and felt fists on the back of his head, his neck. The men shouted abuse while they kicked and punched their victim. They left him bleeding and screaming in the middle of the road.[32]

The victim told journalists that he had believed New Zealand was a safe and tolerant nation. 'The racist language of his attackers had upset him as much as their fists,' the *Spinoff* reported. He asked: 'What makes them have so much anger inside them that they beat someone, hate someone who is not a part of their community? What makes them feel that they should do this?'[33] A peace march was held in Sandringham a few days later in protest against this attack.

Kiwi-Indian children are also targets of physical and verbal

Brothers right about racism

viewpoint

A young Indian man walking home one night is viciously kicked and punched, sworn at and racially abused.

The beating could have been administered because he was Indian. It could have been administered by white supremacists.

A reconstruction of the 1992 crime opened last night's *Inside New Zealand* documentary on racism, *Under The Carpet* (TV3).

As documentaries go this one was brutal, sinister, gripping, enlightening and pretty horrible. But as to the level of white supremacy in New Zealand, it was ultimately inconclusive.

Two Indian brothers, friends of the man, were so incensed at his beating that they decided to try to expose the racism that Indians are up against every day in clean, green New Zealand.

They believe Indians are seen as soft targets — they don't fight back — the bottom of the ethnic heap and the ones who have to fill in the "others" category on forms.

The programme documented apparent racist attacks. In the Hutt Valley, near Wellington, almost all Indian dairy owners have been beaten and robbed at least once; in Hamilton there was a series of fire-bombings; a Sikh temple was shot at; swastikas and anti-Indian slogans are common graffiti; crosses are set alight in backyards, Ku-Klux-Klan-style.

The documentary indicated that the police label such incidents as violent but not racist, but the brothers believe they are out-and-out racism.

If others interviewed in the programme reflect the view of many New Zealanders, I would say the brothers are right.

Said a right-wing activist, Colin King Ansell: "There's a general feeling among a lot of New Zealanders now that we are becoming the dustbin of the Pacific, a dumping ground for everyone else's, um, problems, so to speak."

Said a skinhead: "They're filthy people."

The brothers kept digging and managed to make contact with "Arthur," a member of a secret organisation. Arthur was to be interviewed through a white intermediary. He said his group related unemployment to immigration.

"We use Indians as a training ground for our members ... we can stop them coming here by beating people ... it's applied violence."

A Christchurch skinhead was even worse.

He said, patriotically: "Basically we are just standing up for our country . . . we are fighting for our right to be white — oi, oi." He might have thought he sounded noble, but he just sounded sick, and thick.

In the end we did not find out if Arthur represented the group he claimed to, or if the skinheads represented a national front mentality sweeping the country.

But the documentary left no doubt that racism is alive and well and, literally, kicking in New Zealand.

—Catherine Masters

New Zealand Herald, 2 June 1994

violence.[34] In January 2020 in a Dunedin park, boys taunted a nine-year-old Muslim girl by calling her a 'stinky Indian'. They poked her in the back with sticks, threatened her with a fake gun and rubbed dog faeces on her face.

Even more pervasive than physical violence are the myriad forms of casual or covert racism that Kiwi-Indians face in the twenty-first century. Results of a survey by Massey University's marketing department published in 2004 found that 95 per cent of 1300 respondents reported hearing others make racist remarks about new settlers. More than half had seen or heard a migrant being discriminated against at work; half had witnessed it on the street, in shops or on public transport; and 45 per cent had witnessed it from police, courts or councils or in hospitals.[35] Todd Nachowitz's survey of Kiwi-Indians reiterated that between 2008 and 2013, 48.4 per cent of respondents were the target of a discrimination event in Aotearoa, with a substantial 38.8 per cent experiencing this in their own neighbourhood or when 'out and about'.[36]

One of the most insulting and exclusionary questions asked of Kiwi-Indians, or indeed of any immigrant, is, 'Where are you *really* from?' It strikes at the very heart of belonging, and it tests whether, as a nation and society, we are one. Yusef Patel, for instance, is the great-grandson of Kiwi-Indian pioneer Ismail Ahmed Bhikoo. Yusef was born and raised in Auckland, yet when he was a child a teacher asked him where he came from. He replied, 'Herne Bay,' but was asked again, 'No, where are you really from?'[37]

Sir Anand Satyanand has also had his national identity as a Kiwi publicly questioned.[38] On 4 October 2010, broadcaster Paul Henry asked John Key, then prime minister, whether the governor-general was 'even a New Zealander', demanding, 'Are you going to choose

above: This 2010 cartoon by Edwin Ouellette highlights the racist comments made by TVNZ journalist Paul Henry about the then Governor-General Anand Satyanand.

below: Anand Satyanand addressing the Sir Anand Satyanand Lecture, 29 July 2013 — an annual lecture established in 2011 by *Indian Newslink*.

a New Zealander who looks and sounds like a New Zealander this time?' TVNZ initially defended Henry's willingness 'to say the things we quietly think but are scared to say out loud'.[39] At the time, Satyanand was attending the Commonwealth Games in India. Asked by New Zealand media in New Delhi about his reaction to Henry's comments, he calmly responded, 'I'm reliably informed that I was born at Bethany Hospital, 37 Dryden Street, Grey Lynn in Auckland.' After around 1600 complaints were made to TVNZ, Henry was suspended for two months and then resigned from his employment, although he was later re-employed. He did apologise to Satyanand.

The questioning of identity as a 'real New Zealander' has frequently extended to the exclusionary phrase 'go back to your country'. During 12 days in 2009, in 16 incidents, five Indian students in Invercargill were labelled terrorists, racially abused and told to 'leave our country'.[40] In 2017 at a South Auckland storage facility, an angry man punched and sprayed water from a hose at Bikramjit Singh Mattran, a truck driver, after telling Mattran to 'go back to your country'.[41] That same year, Narindervir Singh was tailgated in a road-rage incident in Glen Innes, Auckland, and a man swore, spat and 'mooned' him. After Narindervir spoke in Punjabi the driver mimicked his language, adding, 'Go back to your f***ing own country, cuz.' Narindervir, who had filmed this abuse, posted the video on Facebook and called for a public apology to the Punjabi community.[42]

Similar abuse occurred the following year in a West Auckland school car park. When Avi Jayapuram asked a woman to be gentler after she banged her car door into his vehicle, she yelled at him,[43] and her partner appeared to be preparing for a fight. Jayapuram, who had lived in Aotearoa for 16 years, responded, 'This is as much my country as it is yours.' He called the police, but they failed to arrive.

'Couple Smell a Rental Bias'

'Newly married couple Arun Kaushish and Poonam Kaushish, in search of a rental home in Tauranga, say they've been overlooked by landlords over fears their native Indian cuisine would leave a lingering smell. "They don't like us cooking curry because the smell is not easy to get out of the house. We have everything a person needs to get a rental . . . I have good pay, good reference and good credit . . . but we can't get a house at the moment; we are feeling very sad." A Bay of Plenty real estate agent backed Kaushish's claims his ethnic fare made it harder for him to find a place. The Human Rights Commission said it had from time to time received complaints over assumptions a family or person would cook particular food in rental accommodation. If this led to an inability to rent, it "could be progressed as a discrimination complaint"'.[44]

— *New Zealand Herald*, 5 December 2016

Despite legislation that prohibits discrimination on the basis of race and ethnicity, some Kiwi-Indians continue to be excluded from spaces; most urgently when finding a place to live. As recently as September 2019 advertisements on Trade Me for rental accommodation in Rotorua and Christchurch stipulated that no Indians should apply.[45] The person listing the Christchurch accommodation denied that the exclusion was about race, but said it was because of behaviour — problems she had experienced with Indian flatmates five years ago.

This generalisation amounts to racial or ethnic stereotyping. Kiwi-Indians who have been denied accommodation have pointed to stereotypes such as claims that 'Indians are dirty',[46] or assumptions that cooking Indian cuisine leaves a lingering smell. Indians have also been refused motel accommodation because they might cook curries while on holiday. In 2003, Partha Roychoudhury complained to the *New Zealand Herald* and the Matamata–Piako District Council after his family was denied accommodation on these grounds by a Morrinsville motelier.[47]

When Sandesh Gopal, a software project manager originally from Bangalore, and his friends were refused entry to a bar at Auckland's Viaduct Harbour on New Year's Eve in 2013, he wondered if it was because of his ethnicity.[48] 'Others, white customers, were let in, and the bouncer just couldn't tell us why he stopped us. The racism here is not overt, but it's the small things that make us feel that maybe we are not welcomed.' Only a day before Sandesh's exclusion from the Auckland bar, Neill Andrews, owner of the Famous nightclub in Wellington, had posted on Facebook:

> Just because we don't let groups of creepy Indian rapists into the club doesn't make us racist, they also don't buy alcohol . . . Probably so they can be sober enough to tie up the sack and lift the body into the back of their hybrid taxi, while wearing oversized leather jackets and sports shoes.[49]

Although Andrews removed the posts, brushing them aside by claiming that his comments were a joke, he still maintained that 'young Indian men are a problem. Indian patrons are a problem everywhere.' Dame Susan Devoy, the race relations commissioner, asked people to boycott the club.

In 2004 the results of an Immigration Service study were made public. One in five immigrants had experienced discrimination since they were granted residency, and one in ten had been discriminated against when applying for jobs. The study suggested that discrimination

Karnail Singh: Ordered to remove turban

'When Karnail Singh turned up to a lunch held to recognise his service to the community, he hardly expected to be asked to strip naked. But that's exactly what it felt like for him when staff at the Manurewa Cosmopolitan Club demanded he remove his turban before entering the club. Mr Singh, a Sikh, was set to be acknowledged at the lunch for volunteers in Age Concern's Accredited Visiting Service, which provides regular home visits to isolated older people. But while the other volunteers enjoyed their meal inside the club, Mr Singh was forced to go home because of the issue over his turban. Club staff told him the turban was "headwear" and wearing headwear in the club's bar is against the club rules. He could wear the turban in the club's function room, but he would have to go through the bar to get to it . . . "This is not headwear – this is part of my religion," he says.

'Age Concern executive officer Wendy Bremner was horrified the club would not let Mr Singh enter a function where he was to be thanked for the contribution he makes to the community. She says Age Concern would not have booked the club if they'd known such an issue would arise . . . After the function Mrs Bremner emailed the club to complain. She received no response, so she followed up with a phone call. "All they said to me was: 'We're entitled to our own rules'".'[50]

Two years earlier a Muslim foreign exchange student had been barred from the same club's dining area because she was wearing a hijab. After the incident with Karnail Singh, the Human Rights Commission mediated. Six months later, the *Manukau Courier* ran the headline 'Intolerant social club stuck in racist past'. It reported that at the Cosmopolitan Club's annual general meeting, 75 per cent of 300 attendees voted to maintain the ban on 'hats', and that, according to an anonymous informer, 'many of those attending feared that if we let in people who wear turbans then the next thing you know is that we will also have to let people wear hoodies and balaclavas into the premises'.[51] In 2015, real estate agent Gurpreet Singh was denied entry to the club to have lunch with his colleagues. Although he complained to the police and the Human Rights Commission, the ban was still in place in 2019 when Jagdip Bajwa and Inderjit Singh, both wearing turbans, were refused entry when they went out for a celebratory meal with friends.[52]

Karnail Singh, photographed by Neil Duddy, 2009.

at work was especially experienced by immigrants from South Asia and South East Asia.[53]

Job discrimination has remained a major barrier for Kiwi-Indians, especially for new migrants and temporary migrant workers. Massey University PhD student Robert Khan surveyed skilled and professional Indo-Fijians with a high level of English and familiar with mainstream New Zealand culture. They still found it difficult to secure employment and had limited support from government agencies.[54] A Massey University report in 2011 on Indians in Auckland indicated even more widespread workplace discrimination. Highly educated and fluent English-speaking Indian migrants experienced considerable downward occupational mobility.[55] A participant in the study recalled: 'When I started in the real estate business, [someone] I knew wanted to sell a house. The Kiwi woman wrinkled her nose and said, "I wouldn't list with you."' Three-quarters of participants in the 2011 study had suffered workplace discrimination; a quarter of employers and a third of employees reported 'some discrimination' against Indians in the media.

Todd Nachowitz's 2015 survey also found that 42 per cent of respondents had experienced discrimination either in their workplace or while looking for employment. Some changed their name to one that New Zealanders could pronounce and found that their employment chances improved considerably.[56] Indians, along with Filipinos and Chinese who hold temporary visas — both for essential skills workers or on post-study work visas — are possibly the most vulnerable and precarious migrant populations in contemporary Aotearoa.[57]

This chapter has predominantly documented contemporary instances of violence and casual racism directed towards Kiwi-

Indians since the late twentieth century, when New Zealand liberalised immigration policy and introduced legislation to combat racial, ethnic and other forms of discrimination. Despite the legislative change, politicians and public figures have continued to perpetuate racial stereotypes that have affected all Kiwi-Indians.

Infamously, in 1983 Auckland city councillor Jolyon Firth called Indians 'curry munchers' and 'short changers' when he chaired a licensing authority hearing for an Indian restaurant in Ponsonby.[58] This action prompted the formation in 1985 of the Auckland Ethnic Council (whose first president would be Shantiben Parbhu). Complaints were made to Hiwi Tauroa, the race relations conciliator, who said that Firth's remarks breached the Race Relations Act. Firth retorted, 'New Zealand is going downhill because of the operation of some laws, such as the Race Relations Act.'[59] As recently as June 2020 in Hamilton, a Māori woman was verbally abused by two groups of men for supporting a 'curry candidate' and allowing an election sign for Gaurav Sharma to be erected on her property.[60] During the previous election campaign, another of Sharma's volunteers (a Pākehā) was asked questions reminiscent of Paul Henry's infamous remarks about the governor-general: 'Could you not find a candidate who looks like a New Zealander?' Sharma was also alarmed that 'some people refused to shake my hand . . . because my skin tone did not match theirs. [They've said] "I'm going to release my dog on you" so I would just leave.'[61] He said there was so much abuse directed at him that his team stopped informing him of it.

In 2018, National Party leader Simon Bridges privately discussed the value of Indian politicians within their party with former member of Parliament Jami-Lee Ross.[62] Ross had stated: 'Two Chinese would be more valuable than two Indians, I have to say,' and Bridges replied, 'Yeah, which is what we've got at the moment, right?'

At the time, the National Party was in Opposition under a Labour-led coalition government. But Shane Jones, a parliamentarian within coalition partner New Zealand First, still targeted Indian immigrants via marriage and education visas. In late 2019

Immigration New Zealand tightened the partnership visa category, insisting that couples were eligible only if they had lived together. This made it difficult for Indians with arranged marriages to bring to New Zealand spouses with whom they had not yet cohabited.[63] Jones told Radio New Zealand: 'You have no legitimate expectations in my view to bring your whole village to New Zealand, and if you don't like it and you're threatening to go home, then catch the next flight home.'[64] Within a fortnight of Jones' diatribe, the category of 'culturally arranged marriage visitor's visa' was established for prospective marriage partners of New Zealanders. This could include those with a marriage that had been culturally arranged outside New Zealand — but Immigration New Zealand still had the final say on what was considered culturally arranged.

This contemporary surveillance of arranged marriages disregards the long history, dating to at least the 1920s, between Indians in Aotearoa and their kin in India and other centres of the Indian diaspora. But once the partnership visa category became politicised, Vision NZ, a party launched by Destiny Church leaders, took the rhetoric further. Leader Hannah Tamaki targeted Kiwi-Indians and any concept of an inclusive nation: 'They are not us and we are not them.' Vision NZ would 'put Kiwis first and immediately stop the phony Indian marriage scheme before proceeding to bring an immediate stop to all further mosques, temples and other foreign buildings of worship being erected in our country. They can be us if they choose to integrate with our Kiwi way of life and not the other way around.'[65]

Jones continued to target Indian immigrants. In late February 2020 he claimed that Indian students had 'ruined' New Zealand's academic institutions.[66] This preposterous and insulting statement clearly generalised about the quality of tertiary institutions and the diverse backgrounds of Kiwi-Indian students. On 3 March, Winston Peters asserted that the comments could not have been racist because they 'come from the Indian people themselves', a claim rejected by several Indian leaders.[67] Narendra Bhana, president of the Auckland Indian Association, responded: 'Shane Jones' comments on Indian students are racist. Period. I simply do not understand why Shane Jones, backed by NZ First, targets the Indian community again and again.' Musician, writer and activist Lizzie Marvelly offered one answer:

> I suspect it's likely that Jones' comments about the Indian community have been intended as dog whistles for those in the electorate who are looking for a scapegoat to blame for a rapidly changing world, or someone to give them permission to be racist. To those who are picking up the overtones, I'm sure Jones' comments will be music to their ears.[68]

Other critical analysis has stressed the role that the media has played in casting Indian migrants as the problem and accusing them of 'lacking the moral values that define (white) New Zealand'.[69] We have seen that othering Indians and questioning their morality was common within racist discourse, notably that of the print media, even when Indian migrants were the targets of discrimination.

From January 2020, in the wake of the panic generated by Covid-19, there were many reports of Chinese and other Asian people in Aotearoa experiencing racism and xenophobia. From 25 March until 27 April 2020 the nation was placed under stringent lockdown measures. By 9 May the Human Rights Commission had received over 250 Covid-19–related complaints; 34 per cent were race-related, and the majority of the targets were of 'Asian/Chinese' descent. Indians were the second-highest target community, and Muslims constituted 28 per cent of such complaints.[70] Evidence that the virus originated from Wuhan in China added fuel to the vitriolic

Meng Foon: Race Relations Commissioner condemns statements against Indian communities

'Shane Jones' continued racist and ignorant statements against Indian communities must stop. As a leader in Government, his words are irresponsible and harmful to many Indian, migrant, and ethnic communities. These types of comments divide us as a country and embolden those that hold racist and xenophobic views.

'This stereotyping goes against the central Māori value of manaakitanga (hospitality), which so many of us love about New Zealand, and is the reason a lot of us came here. International students, including those who come from India, choose New Zealand tertiary education because we are a safe country to study in. They do not deserve to be vilified or discriminated against.

'The comments about Indian students, and others he has made, undermine the rich contributions that the Indian community has made since first arriving here in the mid-1800s. Indian New Zealanders enlisted in WW1 and fought alongside fellow Kiwis at Gallipoli, Somme and Passchendaele. Today, Indian New Zealanders remain an important part of who we are as a society. This month, New Zealand will mark two important events, the one year anniversary of the Christchurch Mosque shootings and Race Relations Day, that remind us of the ugliness of racism and hate. Shane Jones' comments are an affront to these important moments when New Zealanders should be coming together to support one another. . . .

'In an election year, leaders must stop using minorities as their whipping post. We must and can do better. I call upon all New Zealanders and leaders to give nothing to racism and xenophobia.'[71]

— New Zealand Human Rights Commission, 3 March 2020

anti-Chinese hysteria, but this hardly accounts for why Indians and Muslims were targets in a country with minimal levels of Covid-19 cases and where Prime Minister Ardern repeatedly implored the nation to be empathetic and tolerant.

A plan in July 2020 for selected hotels in the South Island to manage isolation facilities for returning New Zealand citizens and residents prompted National parliamentarian Hamish Walker to claim that up to 11,000 people 'are possibly heading for Dunedin, Invercargill and Queenstown from India, Pakistan and Korea'.[72] His comments were condemned by Cabinet minister Megan Woods as 'disgraceful and reprehensible', and also 'misleading'. 'He is scare-mongering and is frankly being racist,' she added. 'The returning New Zealanders he is trying to whip up a public frenzy about are citizens and permanent residents who must stay somewhere safe to ensure that Covid-19 is not spread in the community.' The Indian and Korean communities reiterated how Walker's remarks could spread to more general exclusion against Asians: 'When you say such a thing, the people from India, Pakistan and Korea receive looks of despise, rude encounters at shops, schools, and within their own communities where they live and contribute just like everyone.'[73]

Netsafe New Zealand reported a 238 per cent increase in online hate speech in 2020 from the last six months of 2019. Deputy Police Commissioner Wally Haumaha believed that the pandemic had fuelled racial hate crimes, and at least 92 per cent of those reported to police were 'motivated by an attack on a person's race, their ethnicity'.[74] Chinese were especially targeted, but Meng Foon noted that, since Covid-19, 'these racial stereotypes have led to vitriol like "go back to your country", hurled at anyone who "looks Asian"'.[75]

Although the massacre of 51 people in Christchurch on 15 March 2019 was one of New Zealand's 'darkest days', Shila Nair argued that, 'With the outbreak of Covid-19, we are continuing to experience darker days. When we need to unite, racism appears to have become a deterrent. Our country continues to stumble in the dark, choosing to blink its way through racism, when what is needed is a brutal awakening of our consciousness as a nation.'[76]

The public pushback against contemporary racism emerged as early as 1997, when Race Relations Conciliator Dr Rajen Prasad called on New Zealand to declare 'a war on racism'. He was galvanised to take this action after the attacks on a Pakistani woman and her baby and a Nigerian man in Christchurch, and on an elderly woman in Hawke's Bay. Prasad stated:

> These ugly incidents are the extreme end of racist behaviour that has grown noticeably worse with the spread of the skinhead 'culture' and its half-baked neo-Nazi thinking. It is behaviour that has to be curtailed for the good of all New Zealanders . . . Most New Zealanders are decent and kind people, with a strong sense of fair play — and that makes the emergence of mindless racism all the more dangerous. It is taking hold without much notice being paid, and only incidents such as those reported this week force us to see the unwelcome reality. Many lesser but distressing examples of racial taunting and other unpleasantness are occurring, in our own district, as well as the larger centres.[77]

Twenty years later, in 2017, the New Zealand Human Rights Commission spearheaded the campaign 'Give Nothing to Racism'. The campaign sought to promote awareness of casual and everyday racism and was fronted and directed by film-maker and actor Taika Waititi.[78]

Multicultural councils in New Zealand have sometimes been vocal in combating racism against Kiwi-Indians. When advertisements for rental accommodation in Rotorua and Christchurch posted on Trade Me in September 2019 stated that no Indians should apply, Dr Margriet Theron, president of the Rotorua

Multicultural Council, condemned them as 'racist and unacceptable. It is not who we are . . . It is stereotyping, which is just wrong.'[79]

The 2017 HRC campaign was relaunched in 2020 with a different slogan — 'Racism Is No Joke' — in response to increasing attacks on the Asian community.[80] This time the Auckland-based Filipino comedian James Roque asked the public to stop spreading so-called jokes about the Asian community and Covid-19. 'We're targeting what we like to call the soft middle, which is people who we genuinely believe are good people but maybe think a bit of casual racism isn't actually hurting anyone — when in reality it's hurting a lot of people.'

Poster from the New Zealand Human Rights Commission's 2017 'Give Nothing to Racism' campaign.

From left: Henry Beattie, Harjit Singh, Kevin Gunther and chef Jasram at the Foxton Tasman Fish and Café after new owner Harjit suffered a racist verbal attack from a customer. Gunther, the previous owner, stepped in to help, alerting the press to the incident.

Meng Foon stated in July 2000 that Kiwis don't believe racism is widespread here. 'We are kidding ourselves. . . . those people that say that they aren't racist . . . need to put themselves into the shoes of those people who are being abused.'[81]

While many New Zealanders simply turn a blind eye to instances of racism, some individuals have taken action. In 2019, after a young woman told a Wellington train passenger who was speaking in Hindi on a phone to 'go back to your country, don't speak that language here,' J. J. Philips, the train conductor, ordered the woman to disembark from the train at the next station.[82] That same year, after Harjit Singh, the new owner of the Tasman Fish and Cafe in Foxton, was verbally abused by a customer, former shop owner Kevin Gunther contacted the *Horowhenua Chronicle* to report what he considered blatant racism. The customer had burst into a 'vicious, obscene, racist diatribe' directed at Singh as he was cooking him a burger. 'He said to him, "Don't you touch my food with your dirty slimy hands."'[83]

Since the terrorist attack of 15 March 2019, there has been an outpouring of 'saying no to racism' in Aotearoa. Neelufah Hannif, who had emigrated to New Zealand from Fiji aged nine, and was once called a 'curry muncher' and felt too uncomfortable to wear a hijab to work, told media 10 days after the Christchurch massacre that 'New Zealanders have shown solidarity and it's comforting to know we are "one" and people are there for us'.[84] Yet this chapter has documented the continuation of exclusion and racial hatred for Kiwi-Indians since 15 March — leaving unanswered the question whether we are indeed 'one', and whether the nation has really come to terms with an uncomfortable history of racism, discrimination and exclusion for so many of its peoples.

Now is the time to shatter the invisibility of Kiwi-Indians from Aotearoa's history and to acknowledge not only Indians as settlers within our nation but also the hardships and discrimination they have faced —and still do today.

Notes

List of abbreviations

AJHR	*Appendix to the Journals of the House of Representatives*
ANZ	Archives New Zealand Te Rua Mahara o te Kāwanatanga, Wellington
AS	*Auckland Star*
FT	*Franklin Times*
HRC	New Zealand Human Rights Commission
IW	*Indian Weekender*
KKK	Ku Klux Klan
NZH	*New Zealand Herald*
NZICA	New Zealand Indian Central Association
NZPD	*New Zealand Parliamentary Debates*
ODT	*Otago Daily Times*
RSA	Returned Soldiers' Association

Chapter one. The Indian Diaspora and Exclusion

1. Giselle Byrnes and Catharine Coleborne, 'Editorial Introduction: The Utility and Futility of "The Nation" in Histories of Aotearoa New Zealand,' *New Zealand Journal of History* 45, no. 1 (April 2011): 4.
2. For example, Sylvia Pack, Keith Tuffin and Antonia Lyons, 'Accounts of Blatant Racism Against Māori in Aotearoa New Zealand,' *Sites. A Journal of Social Anthropology and Cultural Studies* 13, no. 2 (2016): 85–110.
3. The number of deaths was later revised to 51.
4. Waikaremoana Waitoki, '"This Is Not Us": But Actually, It Is. Talking About When to Raise the Issue of Colonisation,' *New Zealand Journal of Psychology (Online)* 48, no. 1 (2019): 140, https://researchcommons.waikato.ac.nz/handle/10289/12680
5. Moana Jackson, 'The Connection Between White Supremacy and Colonisation,' *E-Tāngata*, 24 March 2019, https://e-tangata.co.nz/comment- and-analysis/the-connection-between- white-supremacy/
6. See Gautam Ghosh and Jacqueline Leckie, eds., *Asians and the New Multiculturalism in Aotearoa New Zealand* (Dunedin: Otago University Press, 2015), especially the chapters: Camille Nakhid and Heather Devere, 'Negotiating Multiculturalism and the Treaty of Waitangi,' 61–89; and Paul Spoonley, '"I Made a Space For You": Renegotiating National Identity and Citizenship in Contemporary Aotearoa New Zealand,' 39–60.
7. Speech at unveiling of memorial to Edward Peters, Glenore, 12 April 2009.
8. He qualifies this by adding that 'their story challenges several discursive planks on which New Zealand national identity was being constructed in the late nineteenth and early twentieth centuries'. Sekhar Bandyopadhyay, 'A History of Small Numbers: Indians in New Zealand, 1890–1930,' *New Zealand Journal of History* 43, no. 2 (October 2009): 163.
9. The term Kiwi-Indians is not accepted by all people of Indian heritage in Aotearoa and it can impose a problematic homogeneity. See Sekhar Bandyopadhyay, 'Reinventing Indian Identity in Multicultural New Zealand,' in Henry Johnson and Brian Moloughney, eds., *Asia in the Making of New Zealand* (Auckland: Auckland University Press, 2006), 140–6.
10. See TV3 documentary 'Under the Carpet,' *Inside New Zealand*, 31 June 1994.
11. See, for example, critical comments about racism among Indians by Shila Nair, a former journalist from India, and in 2020 a senior advisor with Shakti NZ, an organisation serving migrant and refugee women of

Asian, African and Middle Eastern origin. Shila Nair, 'Of Racism and Coronavirus,' *IW*, 9 May 2020, https://www.indianweekender.co.nz/Pages/ArticleDetails/51/12294/Comment/Of-Racism-and-Coronavirus#; Francis Collins and Christina Stringer, 'Temporary Migrant Worker Exploitation In New Zealand, Report to Ministry of Business, Innovation and Employment, July 2019,' for research and a nuanced discussion of the broader systemic discrimination that engenders the exploitation of temporary Indian migrants. https://www.mbie.govt.nz/dmsdocument/7109-temporary-migrant-worker-exploitation-in-new-zealand

12. See Manying Ip and Jacqueline Leckie, '"Chinamen" and "Hindoos": Beyond Stereotypes to Kiwi Asians,' in Paola Voci and Jacqueline Leckie, eds., *Localizing Asia in Aotearoa* (Wellington: Dunmore Publishing, 2011), 77–106; Nigel Murphy, '"Maoriland" and "Yellow Peril": Discourses of Maori and Chinese in the Formation of New Zealand's National Identity,' in Manying Ip, ed., *The Dragon and the Taniwha: Maori and Chinese in New Zealand* (Auckland: Auckland University Press, 2009), 56–88; Manying Ip, 'Chinese Immigration to Australia and New Zealand: Government Policies and Race Relations,' in T. Chee-Beng, ed., *Routledge Handbook of the Chinese Diaspora*, (Abingdon, UK: Routledge, 2013), 156–175.

13. See 'Poll Tax on Chinese Immigrants Abolished,' NZ History (Ministry for Culture and Heritage, updated 23 September 2020), https://nzhistory.govt.nz/poll-tax-on-chinese-immigrants-abolished

14. Before India and Pakistan became independent states in 1947, colonial India was divided into the provinces of British India and princely states — where Britain ruled indirectly through local rulers. People born in princely states were British Protected Persons, not British subjects, and technically they were stateless. If they had emigrated to New Zealand before 1948 they could be deemed aliens and they had to apply for naturalisation before being eligible for New Zealand citizenship. Some Gujaratis came from the princely states of Baroda and Satchin in the former Rewakantha Agency, while a few Punjabis were from Kapurthala. British Protected Persons could register as citizens of India or Pakistan after independence.

15. *Proclamation by the Queen in Council to the Princes, Chiefs and People of India* (published by the governor-general, Allahabad, 1 November 1858), London. https://www.bl.uk/collection-items/proclamation-by-the-queen-in-council-to-the-princes-chiefs-and-people-of-india

16. Todd Nachowitz, 'Identity and Invisibility: Early Indian Presence in Aotearoa New Zealand, 1769–1850,' in Sekhar Bandyopadhyay and Jane Buckingham, eds., *Indians and the Antipodes: Networks, Boundaries, and Circulation* (New Delhi: Oxford University Press, 2018), 27.

17. Nachowitz, 'Identity and Invisibility,' 46.

18. Ibid., 29.

19. Anne Salmond, *Between Worlds: Early Exchanges Between Maori and Europeans 1773–1815* (Auckland: Penguin, 1997), 235, 290–2.

20. Peter Entwistle, *Taka: A Vignette Life of William Tucker 1784–1817: Convict, Sealer, Trader in Human Heads, Otago Settler, New Zealand's First Art Dealer* (Dunedin: Port Daniel Press, 2005), 103–6.

21. Bishop Selwyn's notes, *Census of People Living at Ruapuke and Stewart Island, Feb 1844*, in Appendix J, Basil Howard, *Rakiura: A History of Stewart Island, New Zealand* (Dunedin: A. H. & A. W. Reed, 1974 [1940]), 379. Ian Smith noted that eight lascars died during attacks on two gangs from the *Matilda* in 1813–14 and that there were several Indian sealers at Whareakeake in 1817, in *Pākehā Settlements in a Māori World New Zealand Archaeology, 1769–1860* (Wellington: Bridget Williams Books, 2020), 92–3.

22. *ODT*, 24 June 1875, 3; Abdullah Martin Drury, 'Once Were Mahometans: Muslims in the South Island of New Zealand, Mid-19th to Late 20th Century, with Special Reference to Canterbury' (MPhil thesis, University of Waikato, 2016), 25, https://hdl.handle.net/10289/10630

23. 'Death of Black Peter,' *Otago Witness*, 29 June 1893, 18, https://paperspast.natlib.govt.nz/newspapers/OW18930629.2.48

24. Denis Dwyer, 'Tuapeka's Obscure Prospector,' *ODT*, 6 November 1990,

18; Jacqueline Leckie, 'Indians in the South Pacific: Recentred Disaporas,' in Jacob Edmond, Henry Johnson and Jacqueline Leckie, eds., *Recentring Asia: Histories, Encounters, Identities* (Leiden: Global Oriental/Brill, 2011), 54–9; Alan Williams, *Edward Peters (Black Peter): The Discoverer of the First Workable Goldfield in Otago* (Balclutha: Clutha Print, 2009).

25. Information about his ancestors kindly supplied by Craig Giddens.

26. See Jacqueline Leckie, 'They Sleep Standing Up: Gujaratis in New Zealand to 1945' (PhD thesis, University of Otago, 1981), http://hdl.handle.net/10523/9118; Jacqueline Leckie, *Indian Settlers: The Story of a New Zealand South Asian Community* (Dunedin: Otago University Press, 2007); Jacqueline Leckie, 'A Long Diaspora: Indian settlement in Aotearoa/New Zealand,' in Sekhar Bandyopadhyay, ed., *India in New Zealand: Local Identities, Global Relations* (Dunedin: Otago University Press, 2010), 45–63; W. H. McLeod, *Punjabis in New Zealand: A History of Punjabi Migration 1890–1940* (Amritsar: Guru Nanak Dev University, 1986).

27. For an excellent account, see Ann Beaglehole, *Refuge New Zealand: A Nation's Response to Refugees and Asylum Seekers* (Dunedin: Otago University Press, 2013), 63–75. During the early 1970s I observed in my dissertation that there was a flurry of anti-Indian letters to newspapers when the Labour government proposed to accept Ugandan refugees, in contrast to the National government's enthusiasm to accept white Rhodesian refugees from Zimbabwe. See Jacqueline Williams, 'A Study of the Gujarati Community in New Zealand Against the Background of Immigration Legislation to 1930' (BA honours dissertation, University of Otago, 1976), 141.

28. Robert L. Khan, 'A Study of Fiji Indian Migrants In New Zealand: Their Migration and Settlement Management and Experiences' (PhD thesis, Massey University, 2011); Jacqueline Leckie, 'Fijians,' *Te Ara — the Encyclopedia of New Zealand* (2015), http://www.TeAra.govt.nz/en/fijians

29. See Beaglehole, *Refuge New Zealand*, 132–8.

30. This information comes mainly from three sources: McLeod, *Punjabis in New Zealand*, 165–7; W. H. McLeod, *A List of Punjabi Immigrants in New Zealand 1890–1939* (Hamilton: Central Indian Association Country Section, 1984); W. H. McLeod and S. S. Bhullar, *Punjab to Aotearoa: Migration and Settlement of Punjabis in New Zealand, 1890–1990* (Hamilton: New Zealand Indian Association Country Section, 1992).

31. Harpreet Singh, 'From Guru Nanak to New Zealand: Mobility in the Sikh Tradition and the History of the Sikh Community in New Zealand to 1947' (PhD thesis, University of Otago, 2016), http://hdl.handle.net/10523/6810

32. Abdullah Martin Drury, 'Mahometans on the Edge of Colonial Empire: Antipodean Experiences.' *Islam and Christian–Muslim Relations* 29, no. 1 (2018): 76.

33. Rafik Patel, 'A Flowing Culture: Images of Early Gujarati Indian-Islamic Migrants in Aotearoa New Zealand' *Transitions: Journal of Transient Migration*, 1, no. 2 (1 June 2017): 251–67.

34. This is based on the author's oral histories with the Bhikoo family; Esup Ismail, Ibrahim Ismail, Mohamad Suliman, 16 October 1977; Mohamad Musa and family, 9 August 1977; Suliaman Ismail Kara and family, November 1977; also Drury, 'Once Were Mahometans'.

35. See Max Towie, 'Deported and Destitute: Indian Students Say New Zealand Failed Them,' *Spinoff*, 2 February 2019, https://thespinoff.co.nz/society/02-02-2019/deported-and-destitute-indian-students-say-new-zealand-failed-them/; Andrew Butcher, 'Immigrants of Doubtful Value: Translating Policy Discourse About International Students in New Zealand,' in Vivienne Anderson and Henry Johnson, eds., *Migration, Education and Translation: Cross-Disciplinary Perspectives on Human Mobility and Cultural Encounters in Education Settings* (Abingdon, UK: Routledge, 2020), 117–118; Education Counts, 'Export Education Levy Statistics', https://www.educationcounts.govt.nz/statistics/international-education/international-students-in-new-zealand; Collins and Stringer, 'Temporary Migrant Worker Exploitation in New Zealand'.

36. See, for example, David C. Atkinson, *The Burden of White Supremacy: Containing Asian Migration in the British Empire and the United States* (Chapel Hill: University of North

Carolina Press, 2016); Robert A. Huttenback, *Racism and Empire: White Settlers and Colored Immigrants in the British Self-Governing Colonies, 1830–1910* (Cornell University Press: Ithaca, NY, 1976), 195–240. For a global survey of the Indian diaspora see Brij V. Lal, Peter Reeves and Rajesh Rai, eds., *The Encyclopedia of the Indian Diaspora* (Singapore: Éditions Didier Millet/ National University of Singapore, 2006).

37. *Times* (London), 12 November 1895.

38. Lala Lajpat Rai, *The Story of My Life: An Unknown Fragment* (edited with an introduction and notes by Joginder Singh Dhanki) (New Delhi: Gitanjali Prakashan, 1978), 42, cited in Sherally Munshi, 'Immigration, Imperialism, and the Legacies of Indian Exclusion,' *Yale Journal of Law and the Humanities* 28, no. 1 (2015): 54, https://digitalcommons.law.yale.edu/yjlh/vol28/iss1/2

39. See Surendra Bhana and Bridglal Pachai, eds., *A Documentary History of Indian South Africans* (Cape Town: New Africa Books, 1984), https://www.sahistory.org.za/archive/documentary-history-indian-south-africans-edited-surendra-bhana-and-bridglal-pachai

40. Huttenback, *Racism and Empire*, 240.

41. See Sushma Raj, 'Australia: 1901 and After,' in Brij Lal, Peter Reeves and Rajesh Rai, eds., *The Encyclopedia of the Indian Diaspora*, 383–5. Note that Māori were excluded from the White Australia policy.

42. McLeod, *Punjabis in New Zealand*, 24.

43. Singh, 'From Guru Nanak to New Zealand,' 147.

44. Munshi, 'Immigration, Imperialism, and the Legacies of Indian Exclusion,' 52, explores the significance of the *Komagata Maru* affair in closing borders for Indian immigrants in Canada, the United States and white-settler countries.

45. See Erika Lee, 'The "Yellow Peril" and Asian Exclusion in the Americas', *Pacific Historical Review* 76 (2007): 537–62.

46. 'Legislation and Constitutional Affairs — Nationality — Indian citizenship,' ACIE 8798 R18873850, EA1, Record no. 159/2/25/part 1a, ANZ.

47. Keith Sinclair, *A History of New Zealand* (Harmondsworth: Penguin, 1959); Keith Sinclair, 'Why Are Race Relations in New Zealand Better Than in South Africa, South Australia or South Dakota?', *New Zealand Journal of History* 5, no. 2 (October 1971): 121–27.

48. James Belich, *Paradise Reforged: A History of the New Zealanders from the 1880s to the Year 2000* (Honolulu: University of Hawai'i Press, 2001); Michael King, *The Penguin History of New Zealand* (Auckland: Penguin, 2003); Giselle Byrnes, *The New Oxford History of New Zealand* (Melbourne: Oxford University Press, 2009).

49. Erik Olssen, 'Towards the Ideal Society.' In Judith Binney, Judith Bassett and Erik Olssen, eds., *The People and the Land / Te Tangata Me Te Whenua* (Wellington: Bridget Williams Books, 2018), 244.

50. See also James Bennett, 'Maori as Honorary Members of the White Tribe,' *Journal of Imperial and Commonwealth History* 29, no. 3 (2001): 33–54.

51. Murphy, '"Maoriland" and "Yellow Peril",' 62. See also Philippa Mein-Smith, *A Concise History of New Zealand* (Cambridge: Cambridge University Press, 2005), 118.

52. Murphy, '"Maoriland" and "Yellow Peril",' 63; Jacqueline Leckie, 'In Defence of Race and Empire: The White New Zealand League at Pukekohe,' *New Zealand Journal of History* 19, no. 2 (1985): 103–29.

53. Rai, cited in Munshi, 'Immigration, Imperialism, and the Legacies of Indian Exclusion,' 54. See also Marilyn Lake and Henry Reynolds, *Drawing the Global Colour Line: White Men's Countries and the International Challenge of Racial Equality* (Carlton: Melbourne University Publishing, 2008); Adam McKeown, *Melancholy Order: Asian Migration and the Globalization of Borders* (New York, NY: Columbia University Press, 2008).

54. Murphy, '"Maoriland" and "Yellow Peril",' 81.

55. Steve Matthewman, 'Pākehā Ethnicity. The Politics of White Privilege,' in Avril Bell, Vivienne Elizabeth, Tracey McIntosh and Matt Wynyard, eds., *A Land of Milk and Honey? Making Sense of Aotearoa New Zealand* (Auckland: Auckland University Press, 2017), 60–7.

56. W. E. B. Du Bois, *The Souls of Black Folk* (New York, NY: New American Library, 1903), 3.

57. Murphy, '"Maoriland" and "Yellow Peril",' 61.

58. For concepts related to race and racism see Amy Elizabeth Ansell, *Race and Ethnicity: The Key Concepts* (Abingdon, UK: Routledge, 2013), and Marvin Harris, *Patterns of Race in the Americas* (Westport, CT: Greenwood Press, 1980).

59. Elaborated by Angelique Nairn, 'What Is with All the Hate? A Thematic Analysis of New Zealanders' Attitudes to the Human Rights Commission's "Give Nothing to Racism" Social Marketing Campaign,' *New Zealand Sociology* 35, no. 1 (2020): 97–122.

60. More extensive narratives can be found in Robyn Andrews, 'Did You Know Your Great Grandmother Was an Indian Princess? Early Anglo Indian Arrivals in New Zealand,' in Sekhar Bandyopadhyay and Jane Buckingham, eds., *Indians and the Antipodes: Networks, Boundaries, and Circulation* (New Delhi: Oxford University Press, 2018), 210–32; Drury, 'Once Were Mahometans'; Rebecca Lal and Vasanti Unka, eds., *With a Suitcase of Saris. From India to Aotearoa: Stories of Pioneer Indian Women* (Auckland: Aditi Indian Women's Collective, My Sunroom, 2016); Leckie, *Indian Settlers;* Jane McCabe, *Kalimpong Kids: The New Zealand Story, in Pictures* (Dunedin: Otago University Press, 2020); McLeod, *Punjabis in New Zealand*; Edwina Pio, *Sari: Indian Women at Work in New Zealand* (Wellington: Dunmore Publishing, 2008); Singh, 'From Guru Nanak to New Zealand'.

Chapter two. Immigration, the Backbone of Aotearoa New Zealand

1. See Peter O'Connor, 'Keeping New Zealand White, 1908–1920,' *New Zealand Journal of History* 11, no. 1 (1968): 41–65; Further details of the act are provided in Leckie, 'They Sleep Standing Up,' 241–47; 342–52; 371–82.

2. Belich, *Paradise Reforged*, 232.

3. Ravjibhai Hira, interviewed by the author, 31 January 1976. Customary or respectful additions to names are used throughout this book, but not always. Thus Ravji Hira was known as Ravjibhai (bhai in Gujarati meaning brother). Ben (sister) is a respectful way of referring to a woman within Gujarati culture. Other regions and cultural groups within India had different traditions of naming and respect.

4. Kanu Makan, personal communication, 2004.

5. McLeod, *Punjabis in New Zealand*, 41.

6. McLeod and Bhullar, *Punjab to Aotearoa*, 20.

7. New Zealand Political Reform League, *Handbook for Reform Party Candidates (*Wellington: Wright and Carman, 1914).

8. J. K. Natali and Khusal Madhu, interviewed by the author, 1977–78.

9. McLeod, *Punjabis in New Zealand*, 100. Joala's photograph is in chapter 5 of this book.

10. *NZ Truth*, 6 January 1912, 1, https://paperspast.natlib.govt.nz/newspapers/NZTR19120106.2.2

11. *NZPD* 187 (11 August 1920): 84.

12. Immigration Restriction Amendment Act 1920, An Act to amend the Immigration Restriction Act, 1908. 1920, no. 23.

13. Murphy, 'Report on Indian Community Grievances,' 15.

14. *New Zealand Statutes*, 1920, no. 23, Immigration Restriction Amendment Bill. Gazetted on 13 January 1921.

15. *NZPD* 187: 920.

16. *New Zealand Statutes*, 1920, 23(5), (1)(2).

17. Abdullah Drury, 'Don't Panic: Muslims in the Waikato Region of New Zealand,' *Waikato Islamic Studies Review* 2, no. 10 (2016): 45.

18. *Quick March*, 10 September 1920, 3 no. 29, 57–8.

19. *New Zealand Statutes*, Clause 11. C33/25 (Customs Department) 1921/8, 10 December 1920. Memo from Attorney General to shipping companies. C33/25, 1921/43, 19 April

1921, reiterated that Indians would not be granted verbal permission to land in New Zealand.

20. L/E/7/1192, 1+0 222, 10 December 1920 (India Office Library records, British Museum).

21. C33/25, Memo 1921/8, 21 January 1921, from Comptroller of Customs to shipping companies.

22. For a detailed analysis of Indians' re-entry certificates during the 1920s, see Michael Roche and Sita Venkateswar, 'Indian Migration to New Zealand in the 1920s. Deciphering the Immigration Restriction Amendment Act 1920,' in Sekhar Bandyopadhyay and Jane Buckingham, eds., *Indians and the Antipodes: Networks, Boundaries, and Circulation* (New Delhi: Oxford University Press, 2018), 129–61.

23. Bhanu Daji, 'Ganga Ravji,' in Lal and Unka, *With a Suitcase of Saris,* 34–39.

24. See Leckie, *Indian Settlers,* 90–101.

25. 'Married Nearly 84 years, and Still Going Strong,' 10 February 2019, *Stuff,* https://www.stuff.co.nz/national/110454077/married-nearly-84-years-and-still-going-strong

26. Email to Prithi Pal Singh, 7 February 2020.

27. Document with author, compiled by great-grandchild Sukdeep Singh, 13 July 2004.

28. Hira and Jivan Bava, Ganesh-Sisodra, Gujarat, 1978; Lala Bava, Wellington, 10 December 1977, interviewed by the author.

29. Petition of the NZICA (New Zealand Indian Central Association), Public Petitions M to Z Committee (Reports of the) (Dr. A. M. Finlay, Chairman), *AJHR,* 1947 Session I, I-02, 21 November 1947, Petition No. 76/47, https://paperspast.natlib.govt.nz/parliamentary/AJHR 1947-I.2.4.3.2

30. C33/253M, 'Immigration of Indians'.

31. Memorandum, Labour Dept, H.O. 108660 to Collector of Customs, Auckland, 27 July 1955, noted that Indians of New Zealand citizenship were still approaching the Labour Department for re-entry permits although this was unnecessary.

32. 158/15/1. C.M. (51) (18). Confidential memo from Prime Minister's office to Minister of Immigration, 19 March 1951.

33. Immigration (I) 22/1/134. Memo from Director of Employment to Minister of Immigration, 23 May 1953.

34. Ibid.

35. For example, I 22/1/134, letter from six Punjabis, Taumarunui to Minister of Immigration, 26 January 1953. Deputation from NZICA to Minister of Immigration, 18 March 1953.

36. Ibid., from Prime Minister, to Minister of Immigration, C.M. (57) 25, following Cabinet meeting 1 July 1957.

37. NZICA Conference, *45th Annual Report and Balance Sheet,* 1971.

38. Customs Department memorandums, C 33/1, Memo 33/25/11, 9 April 1951.

39. NZICA to Minister of Immigration, in NZICA, *Annual Report and Financial Statement,* 1956.

40. NZICA Conference, *34th Annual Report and Balance Sheet, 1960.*

41. Sean Brawley, 'No "White Policy" in New Zealand: Fact and Fiction in New Zealand's Asian Immigration Record, 1946–1978,' *New Zealand Journal of History* 27, no. 1 (1993): 16.

42. Memorandum, 'Immigration into New Zealand: International Problems', Department of External Affairs, 1953, PM 323/3/18, Part 1 (ANZ).

43. Ibid.

44. Brawley, 'No '"White Policy",' 17.

45. W. T. Roy, 'Immigration Policy and Legislation,' in Keith Westhead Thomson and Andrew Drago Trlin, eds., *Immigration in New Zealand* (Palmerston North: Massey University, 1970), 15.

46. Murphy, 'Report on Indian Community Grievances,' 37–38.

47. Brawley, 'No White Policy,' 30.

48. This section is mostly from Ann Beaglehole, 'Immigration Regulation — 1946–1985: Gradual Change,' *Te Ara — the Encyclopedia of New Zealand,* published 8 February 2005, updated 18 August 2015, 4–5, http://www.TeAra.govt.nz/en/immigration-regulation/pages-4-5

49. Raman Ganda, personal communication.

50. Information supplied by Manisha Morar, 18 January 2021.

Chapter three. White Race Organisations

1. Uka Chibba, *Indians in Pukekohe 1918–2006* (Pukekohe: Private publication, 2007).
2. See Robert E. Bartholomew, *No Maori Allowed: New Zealand's Forgotten History of Racial Segregation: How a Generation of Māori Children Perished in the Fields of Pukekohe* (Auckland: Robert E. Bartholomew, 2020).
3. As Bartholomew verified in his research on anti-Māori discrimination at Pukekohe. *No Maori Allowed*, 8.
4. Bharat Jamnadas, 'Our Pioneers Did Not Have It So Easy,' *IW*, 24 May 2013, https://www.indianweekender.co.nz/Pages/ArticleDetails/52/3722/Editorials/Our-Pioneers-did-not-have-it-so-easy
5. For example, *Manawatu Standard*, 25 June 1907, 4; 30 July 1908, 5.
6. 'The White Race League', *Otago Witness*, 17 July 1907, 53.
7. 'Racial Purity,' *New Zealand Times*, 1 July 1907, 5.
8. 'Ku Klux Klan,' *AS*, 27 August 1923, 3, https://paperspast.natlib.govt.nz/newspapers/AS19230827.2.13
9. *AS*, 11 December 1923, 1, https://paperspast.natlib.govt.nz/newspapers/AS19231211.2.6. A spokesman for the KKK warned Mr Jolly, a shopkeeper, that four shops would be torched. 'Fire at Mt Eden,' *Gisborne Times*, 12 December 1923, 6, https://paperspast.natlib.govt.nz/newspapers/GIST19231212.2.41. See also Scott Hamilton, 'New Zealand's Long and Violent History of Anti-Indian Racism,' *Spinoff*, 27 June 2019, 5, https://thespinoff.co.nz/atea/27-06-2019/prehistory-of-a-beating-new-zealands-violent-anti-indian-past/
10. 'The Ku Klux Klan,' *Ashburton Guardian*, 12 October 1923, 5, https://paperspast.natlib.govt.nz/newspapers/AG19231012.2.50
11. 'The Ku Klux Klan,' *NZH*, 9 October 1923, 6, https://paperspast.natlib.govt.nz/newspapers/NZH19231009.2.48
12. See Diane B. Paul, John Stenhouse and Hamish G. Spencer, eds., *Eugenics at the Edges of Empire New Zealand, Australia, Canada and South Africa* (Cham: Springer International Publishing, 2018).
13. 'Asiatic Problem,' *FT*, 27 November 1925, 4, https://paperspast.natlib.govt.nz/newspapers/FRTIM19251127.2.18.1
14. 'Asiatic Problem,' *FT*, 18 December 1925, 5, https://paperspast.natlib.govt.nz/newspapers/FRTIM19251218.2.24. See Leckie, 'In Defence of Race and Empire.'
15. *FT*, 20 November 1925, 4, https://paperspast.natlib.govt.nz/newspapers/FRTIM19251120.2.15.1
16. 'The Hindus,' *FT*, 18 December 1925, 4, https://paperspast.natlib.govt.nz/newspapers/FRTIM19251218.2.13
17. *FT*, 20 November 1925.
18. 'Miscellaneous — [Asian Immigration] 1916–1944,' AAAC 6015 W4686 R337672, Box 13, Record no. 158/15, Parvin to Bollard 25 March 1926 (ANZ).
19. 'A White N.Z.,' *FT*, 21 June 1926, 4, https://paperspast.natlib.govt.nz/newspapers/FRTIM19260621.2.7
20. *FT*, 18 December 1925, 5.
21. 'White N.Z. League,' *FT*, 20 January 1926, 5, https://paperspast.natlib.govt.nz/newspapers/FRTIM19260120.2.27
22. White New Zealand League, 'Citizens of the Future Are the Children of Today', 1926; 'Don't Fail to Read this Appeal', 1927 (Pukekohe: White New Zealand League), Hocken Collections, Uare Taoka o Hākena, University of Otago.
23. 'Our Asiatics,' *FT*, 18 January 1926, 4, https://paperspast.natlib.govt.nz/newspapers/FRTIM19260118.2.10
24. 'White N.Z. League,' *FT*, 10 November 1926, 5, https://paperspast.natlib.govt.nz/newspapers/FRTIM19261110.2.35
25. 'White New Zealand,' *AS*, 23 January 1926, 8, https://paperspast.natlib.govt.nz/newspapers/AS19260123.2.23
26. For example, borough councils of Petone, Eltham, Ohakune, cited in 'Miscellaneous — [Asian Immigration] 1916–1944,' Parvin to Bollard 25 March 1926.
27. 'A White N.Z.,' *FT*, 24 September 1926, 5, https://paperspast.natlib.govt.nz/newspapers/FRTIM19260924.2.26
28. 'A White N.Z.,' *FT*, 8 July 1927, 5, https://paperspast.natlib.govt.nz/newspapers/FRTIM19270708.2.24
29. Ibid.
30. 'A White N.Z.,' *FT*, 12 November 1928, 5, https://paperspast.natlib.govt.nz/newspapers/FRTIM19281112.2.21
31. 'A White N.Z.,' *FT*, 7 November 1928,

4, https://paperspast.natlib.govt.nz/newspapers/FRTIM19281107.2.7

32. 'A White N.Z.,' *FT*, 12 November 1928, https://paperspast.natlib.govt.nz/newspapers/FRTIM19281112.2.21
33. *AS*, 13 April 1926, 7.
34. Department of Maori Affairs, MA 1929/356, 'Evidence Given Before Committee Investigating Conditions and Accommodation of Maoris Employed in European, Chinese and Asiatic Market Gardens in Auckland and Surrounding Districts,' 144; Quotation from J. W. Gregory, *The Menace of Colour* (London: Seeley, Service & Co, 1925).
35. Barbara Brookes, 'Gender, Work and Fears of a "Hybrid Race" in 1920s New Zealand', *Gender and History* 19, no. 3 (2007): 505–6 outlines Te Akarana Maori Association, founded in Auckland in 1927 by a group of elite Māori men to promote Māori welfare. The association was particularly concerned about racial miscegenation and degradation of Māori through interracial liaisons with Indians or Chinese.
36. 'Chinese Markets,' *FT*, 3 November 1930, 5, https://paperspast.natlib.govt.nz/newspapers/FRTIM19301103.2.25
37. See 'Miscellaneous — [Asian Immigration] 1916–1944,' Record no. 158/15, 1 October 1931.
38. *Evening Post*, 24 September 1932, 14.
39. Ibid.
40. 'Pukekohe Again,' *FT*, 5 October 1932, 5, https://paperspast.natlib.govt.nz/newspapers/FRTIM19321005.2.18
41. 'Slow Strangulation of White Growers,' *FT*, 23 April 1937, 5, https://paperspast.natlib.govt.nz/newspapers/FRTIM19370423.2.28
42. Ibid.
43. *FT*, 25 September 1950.
44. Copies of minutes, Country Section (Hocken Collections, Uare Taoka o Hākena, University of Otago).
45. NZICA Inc., Hamilton, I.S. 1927/28. Constitution.
46. 'Department of Internal Affairs, File on Asian Immigration,' AAAC W4686 6015, Box 13, Record number 158/15 (ANZ).
47. Copy of petition held by NZICA. Note that the New Zealand and India League (who were mostly Europeans) submitted a similar petition, 13 September 1926. See 'Miscellaneous — [Asian Immigration] 1916–1944'.

Chapter four. Discrimination at Work

1. Srinivasa Sastri, 'Report by Right Honourable V. S. Srinivasa Sastri P.C. Regarding his Deputation to Dominions of Australia, New Zealand and Canada,' (Simla: Central Government Press, 1923), New Zealand Department of Internal Affairs file I.A. 13/63/47.
2. *NZPD* 89 (22 August 1895): 349. Reeves speaking on the Asiatic and other Immigration Restriction Bill.
3. 10 (1) of the bill. Available at http://www.nzlii.org/nz/legis/hist_bill/uhpb18961081336/
4. *NZPD* 95 (11 September 1896): 597.
5. Ibid. 'Brummagem' refers to cheap or showy items.
6. 'Fruit Hawkers,' *Sun* (Christchurch), 31 March 1915, 9, https://paperspast.natlib.govt.nz/newspapers/SUNCH19150331.2.74
7. *NZPD* 191: 391.
8. 'How They Live,' *Evening Post*, 15 December 1920. Wellington City Council minutes, 26 August 1918.
9. Wellington City Council minutes, Letter from Town Clerk to H. F. O'Leary (Solicitor for Indians), 29 August 1918.
10. Lalloo Morar, interviewed by the author, December 1977.
11. G. H. Roche, *Waikato Times*, 5 February 1960.
12. Wellington City By-law No. 56 (Amendment) 1927, passed on 8 September, Wellington City Council Archives, By-laws 1908-1929 00251:1:6.
13. Wellington City By-law no. 1 1908, Part XVI.
14. *NZPD* 163 (20 August 1913): 858; 165 (16 October 1913): 766; *Dominion*, 21 August 1913, 5.
15. 2 June 1920, 'Miscellaneous Asian

Immigration, 1916–1944,' AAAC W4658 6015, Box 13, 158/15 (ANZ).

16. *Quick March,* July 1920, 45.

17. *Maoriland Worker,* 1 December 1920.

18. *NZPD* 187 (1920): 912–13.

19. *Maoriland Worker,* 1 December 1920.

20. *Press,* 3 July 1920, 8.

21. *NZPD* 188 (7 October 1920): 351; *Evening Post,* 23 September 1920, 7; *NZH,* 18 October 1920, 4.

22. I + 0 222, 1921, L/E/7/1192 (India Office Records, British Library).

23. 'A Farewell Function, Waimiha,' n.d., c1946 (Natali's memorabilia). See also Jacqueline Leckie, 'Natali, Jelal Kalyanji,' *Dictionary of New Zealand Biography,* first published in 2000, *Te Ara — the Encyclopedia of New Zealand,* https://teara.govt.nz/en/biographies/5n1/natali-jelal-kalyanji (accessed 2 January 2021).

24. *Wairarapa Daily Times,* 7 April 1921, 4.

25. *FT,* 6 May 1921, 4, https://paperspast.natlib.govt.nz/newspapers/FRTIM19210506.2.15.2

26. See Hugh Tinker, 'Odd Man Out: The Loneliness of the Indian Colonial Politician — The Career of Manilal Doctor,' *Journal of Imperial and Commonwealth History* 2, no. 1 (1974): 226–43; *NZH,* 27 November 1920, 9 July 1921, 11 July 1921.

27. 'Report of Committee on Employment of Maoris on Market Gardens, 1929,' *AJHR,* 1929, G -11.

28. Ibid., 5.

29. Department of Maori Affairs, 'Evidence Given Before Committee Investigating Conditions and Accommodation of Maoris,' 85–6.

30. Ibid., 86.

31. 'Franklin Growers Meet Labour Minister,' *FT,* 15 March 1937, 4, https://paperspast.natlib.govt.nz/newspapers/FRTIM19370315.2.14

32. 'Asiatic Influx,' *Evening Post,* 12 July 1920, 2.

33. This account and details of the allegations is sourced from McLeod, *Punjabis in New Zealand,* 172–9. McLeod was writing in 1986, and since then professional ethics in relation to allegations of sexual abuse have changed considerably. It is likely that such a case would be investigated today.

34. 'Asiatic Competition,' *NZH,* 16 June 1920, 7, https://paperspast.natlib.govt.nz/newspapers/NZH19200616.2.79

35. 'The Asiatic Influx,' *NZH,* 26 May 1920, 7, https://paperspast.natlib.govt.nz/newspapers/NZH19200526.2.78

36. 'Our Asiatics,' *FT,* 5 December 1930, 5, https://paperspast.natlib.govt.nz/newspapers/FRTIM19301205.2.16

37. A memorandum to the Minister of Internal Affairs dated 11 November 1930 recommended against any compulsory registration of Asian traders, also pointing out that it was a recognised practice for a firm to start with a fictitious name and that there was no legal requirement for the registration of business names. 'Miscellaneous Asian Immigration, 1916–1944.'

38. Ibid.

39. 'Humiliating,' *Evening Post,* 4 May 1937, 8, https://paperspast.natlib.govt.nz/newspapers/EP19370504.2.53

40. Miscellaneous Asian Immigration, 1916–1944 (ANZ).

41. 'Shires Fruit and Vege Market', https://www.shires.co.nz/history, accessed 2 January 2021.

42. Brian Setford, 'Indian Family Has Made Major Contribution To Dannevirke,' *Evening News,* 22 July 2000, 3. Setford wrote that Chibba arrived in New Zealand in 1915 and that the business was established in 1919, which is different to the history on Shires' website.

43. 'Correspondence,' *FT,* 7 April 1943, 2, https://paperspast.natlib.govt.nz/newspapers/FRTIM19430407.2.8

44. 'Hindu's Rights,' *NZH,* 28 April 1942, https://paperspast.natlib.govt.nz/newspapers/NZH19420428.2.75

45. NZICA, 1961 Annual Conference. Report and Balance Sheet, 3.

46. Leckie, 'They Sleep Standing Up,' 652; *Wellington Indian Association Inc. Golden Jubilee 1925–1976.* Wellington, 1976.

47. Judgement of the Crown Court, October 1944 (Natali's memorabilia).

48. *FT,* 2 June 1943, 3, https://paperspast.natlib.govt.nz/newspapers/FRTIM19430602.2.25

49. *FT,* 29 August 1952; *NZH,* 6 February 1952.

50. I (Immigration), 22/2/234, W. G. Metcalfe to Sullivan, 23 September 1953.

Chapter five. War and Welfare

1. As declared at a meeting of the Franklin RSA, 'Slow Strangulation of White Growers,' *FT*, 23 April 1937, 5, https://paperspast.natlib.govt.nz/newspapers/FRTIM19370423.2.28
2. Michael Roche and Sita Venkateswar, 'Neither Natural-born British Subjects nor Aliens,' in John Crawford, David Littlewood and James Watson, eds., *Experience of a Lifetime: People, Personalities and Leaders in the First World War* (Auckland: Massey University Press, 2016), 151.
3. Ibid, 147.
4. Ibid.
5. Jane McCabe, '"An Ideal Life": Anglo-Indians in the New Zealand Expeditionary Force,' in David Monger, Katie Pickles and Sarah Murray, eds., *Endurance and the First World War: Experiences and Legacies in New Zealand and Australia* (Newcastle: Cambridge Scholars Publishing, 2014), 198.
6. New Zealand Defence Force, Personnel Archives, 'Singh, Weer — WW1 N/N — Army,' R107817716, Series 18805 (ANZ), https://ndhadeliver.natlib.govt.nz/delivery/DeliveryManagerServlet?dps_pid=IE11097493
7. 'Singh, Sham — WW1 16/1553, 'R120550694, Series 18805 (ANZ), https://ndhadeliver.natlib.govt.nz/delivery/DeliveryManagerServlet?dps_pid=IE11232456; Len Kenna and Crystal Jordan, 'Sham Singh New Zealand Army WWI,' 25 April 2015, http://australianindianhistory.com/sham-singh-an-anzac/
8. Thanks to Linda Bryder for this information.
9. *AS*, 19 June 1918, 7.
10. Ella Johnson, 'Soldier Singh, an Indian ANZAC,' Auckland War Memorial Museum Tāmaki Paenga Hira, online cenotaph, first published 1 November 2017, www.aucklandmuseum.com/war-memorial/online-cenotaph/features/soldier-singh-an-indian-anzac
11. Officer Commanding Auckland District to New Zealand Military Forces HQ, Wellington, 25 November 1916, AD1830 29/220 (ANZ).
12. Auckland War Memorial Museum Tāmaki Paenga Hira, online cenotaph; Roche and Venkateswar, 'Neither Natural-born British Subjects nor Aliens,' 142–46.
13. Johnson, 'Soldier Singh'; Roche and Venkateswar, 'Neither Natural-born British Subjects nor Aliens,' 143–46.
14. Johnson, 'Soldier Singh.' Jagt may have referred to Sagt (abbreviation of Sergeant). See Roche and Venkateswar, 144–6.
15. Len Kenna and Crystal Jordan, 'Ratan Chand Mehra, an Anzac,' 25 April 2015, http://australianindianhistory.com/ratan-chand-mehra-an-anzac/
16. Circular M.P. No. 18: To Personnel of Man-Power Committees, 9 October 1940, Papers of George Alexander Monk relating to Wellington Branch of Armed Forces Appeal Board, MS-Papers-7757-01, Alexander Turnbull Library. I am grateful to Dr David Littlewood for supplying information on conscription during World War II, 18 September 2020.
17. 'Asiatics Liable. Territorial Service,' *NZH*, 27 March 1941, 8, https://paperspast.natlib.govt.nz/newspapers/NZH19410327.2.54
18. For example, 'Two Indian Fruiterers', *NZH*, 14 January 1943, 4, https://paperspast.natlib.govt.nz/newspapers/NZH19430114.2.38
19. *ODT*, 13 August 1942, 4, https://paperspast.natlib.govt.nz/newspapers/ODT19420813.2.29
20. 'A Food Problem,' *Gisborne Herald*, 14 March 1942, 5, https://paperspast.natlib.govt.nz/newspapers/GISH19420314.2.96
21. Circular A. B. No. 4: Memorandum for Chairmen, Members, Crown Representatives and Secretaries of Armed Forces Appeal Boards, 27 March 1941, Armed Forces Appeal Board and Manpower Committees — Circulars and Instructions, NS-DN4 1 (ANZ).
22. Auckland War Memorial Museum Tāmaki Paenga Hira, online cenotaph, https://www.aucklandmuseum.com/war-memorial/online-cenotaph/record/C29722?n=Mewa&ordinal=0&from=%2Fwar-memorial%2Fonline-cenotaph%2Fsearch; *AS*, 18 August 1945, 7.
23. *AS*, 21 February 1941, 4.

24. McLeod, *Punjabis in New Zealand,* 150, fn 1.
25. Cited in Tiwari, *Indians in New Zealand,* 17–18.
26. McLeod, *Punjabis in New Zealand,* 19; 21; McLeod, *A List of Punjabi Immigrants in New Zealand,* 139; Kapil Tiwari, ed., *Indians in New Zealand, Studies in a Sub Culture* (Wellington: Price Milburn for the New Zealand Indian Central Association, 1980), 63.
27. Email from Captain Todd Skilton, New Zealand Defence Force, Medals Office to Abdullah Drury, 31 July 2013.
28. *AS,* 11 June 1940, 6.
29. *Evening Post,* 26 January 1940, 9.
30. Tiwari, *Indians in New Zealand,* 17–8.
31. Bates spelled the name as Johnson, whereas the newspapers reported Johnstone.
32. In fact, it was Johnstone who returned to India to serve in the 1857 Indian uprising. He then returned to Waikato and committed suicide.
33. Ibid.
34. 'Qualifications of Asiatics 1904–1936' R398433, series 16143 (ANZ).
35. It is not clear if the writer was referring to Sohman or Nudin. "A Revoked Pension," *Lyttelton Times,* 30 May 1908, 13, https://paperspast.natlib.govt.nz/newspapers/LT19080530.2.123
36. Commissioner of Pensions to Minister of Pensions, 21 July 1908, 'Qualifications of Asiatics 1904–1936.'
37. Internal Affairs Department. IA 116/10, 11 April 1957, cited in Murphy, 'Report on Indian Community Grievances,' 34–5.
38. New Zealand Indian Central Association (Inc), *Annual Conference. Report and Financial Statements,* 44th (1970), 10; 45th (1971), 10; 46th (1972), 8, cited in Murphy, 'Report on Indian Community Grievances,' 39.

Chapter six. Casual and Informal Racism

1. Chester M. Pierce, Jean V. Carew, Diane Pierce-Gonzalez and Deborah Wills, 'An Experiment in Racism: TV Commercials,' *Education and Urban Society* 10, no. 1 (November 1977): 65. See also Derald Wing Sue, *Microaggressions in Everyday Life: Race, Gender, and Sexual Orientation* (Hoboken, NJ: Wiley, 2010). I have drawn upon the theoretical insight and literature review from Angelique Nairn, 'What Is with All the Hate?'
2. Derald Wing Sue et al., 'Racial Microaggression in Everyday Life: Implications for Clinical Practice,' *American Psychologist* 62, no. 4 (2007): 273, cited in Nairn, 'What Is with All the Hate?,' 101.
3. New Zealand Human Rights Commission (HRC), 2017, cited in Nairn, 'What Is with All the Hate?,' 98. See also Indra Prasad, 'Silent Discontent: Experiences of Everyday Racism in New Zealand = He Amuamu Nohopuku: He Whakapātanga Whakatoihara Tangata Ia Rā, Ia Rā, ki Aotearoa' (master's thesis, Victoria University of Wellington, 2000).
4. Waitoki, '"This Is Not Us"', 141.
5. See Paul Spoonley and Walter Hirsh, *Between the Lines: Racism and the New Zealand Media* (Auckland: Heinemann Reed, 1990); Sandy Lee and Trudie Cain, 'Diversity Dividends and the Dehumanisation of Immigrants in the News Media in Aotearoa New Zealand,' *New Zealand Population Review* 45 (2019): 185–210.
6. *NZ Truth,* 19 March 1910, 6. Sali Mahomet='s ethnic origins are uncertain. He and his father Sultan Mohamet were described, and have described themselves, as Assyrian, Indian and Ceylonese (Sri Lankan). Drury, 'Mahometans on the Edge,' 84.
7. *NZ Truth,* 6 March 1909, 6.
8. *NZ Truth,* 13 January 1912, 5.
9. 'Unpopular Hindus,' NZH, 9 July 1920, 4, https://paperspast.natlib.govt.nz/newspapers/NZH19200709.2.25?items_per_page=10&phrase=2&query=forcibly+ejected+from+the+town&snippet=true
10. Virginia Winder, 'Singi Moral: A Fruitful Life,' Puke Ariki, created 24 March 2004, accessed 19 January 2021, https://

terangiaoaonunui.pukeariki.com/all-stories/taranaki-stories/singi-moral-a-fruitful-life/

11. *AS*, 17 July 1922, 7; 22 July 1922, 12.

12. Lalbhai Patel, Auckland, 19 July 1977; Maganbhai Ranchhod, Pukekohe, 17 September 1977; Keshav Parsot, Pukekohe, 11 February 1978; Dayalbhai Kesry, Papakura, 1977–81, interviewed by the author. See also Bartholomew, *No Maori Allowed*; B. Kernot, *People of the Four Winds* (Wellington: Hicks, Smith & Sons, 1972), 12. These practices came to the attention of the government of India. See F. S. Bajpai, Secretary to Government of India, to Under-Secretary of State for India, Economic & Overseas Department, 1 December 1932, I. O. F436/ 32, India Office, London; forwarded by J. H. Thomas, Secretary of State for Dominion Affairs, to Lord Bledisloe, Government House, New Zealand, regd no. 326, no. 19, 1933.

13. *Bay of Plenty Beacon*, 2 February 1945, 8, https://paperspast.natlib.govt.nz/newspapers/BPB19450202.2.38

14. A. R. M., 'Get Rid of Haining Street!,' *New Zealand Observer*, 11 February 1937, 10–11.

15. Verified by Bartholomew, *No Maori Allowed.*

16. Wellington Indian Sports Club, *Wellington Indian Sports Club: The First 50 years 1935–1985* (Wellington: Zodiac Printing, 1985), 7; Leckie, 'They Sleep Standing Up', 615.

17. 'Menace of Hindus,' *Waikato Times*, 24 February 1920, 5.

18. NZICA, *Report and Financial Statement*, 1952, Christchurch; 1953, Auckland.

19. *Northern Advocate*, 9 September 1949, 4, https://paperspast.natlib.govt.nz/newspapers/NA19490909.2.30

20. Letter from J. K. Natali, to Chairman and Members, Royal Licensing Commission, Waimiha, 4 July 1945; 'Report of the Royal Commission on Licensing.' *AJHR*, 1946, 4, H-38, 144–5.

21. *Franklin County News* (Franklin A & P Show Centenary Supplement), 1986, 70.

22. Motiram's son, Ramonbhai, interviewed by the author at Pukekohe in 1977. See Chibba, *Indians in Pukekohe*, 79–80; Leckie, *Indian Settlers*, 59. Note different spellings of Vallabh/Wallabh. 'Assault alleged,' *FT*, 19 July 1933, 5, https://paperspast.natlib.govt.nz/newspapers/FRTIM19330719.2.18; 'A Civil Action,' *FT*, 2 August 1933, 4, https://paperspast.natlib.govt.nz/newspapers/FRTIM19330802.2.15

23. Nairn, 'What Is with All the Hate?,' 101–2, also cites the literature that has argued this perspective and the wide range of effects on those subjected to microaggression.

24. Winder, 'Singi Moral.'

25. Mandrika Rupa, interviewed by Jack Perkins, 'The Quarter Acre Indians,' Spectrum Radio, 997 (Wellington: National Radio), 14 February 1998.

26. Grandson, Mohammed Ebrahim Musa, interviewed by Jacqueline Leckie, 1977.

27. McLeod, *Punjabis in New Zealand*, 159.

28. Nayna Bhana (daughter of Nandiben), personal communication, 2004.

29. Rafik Patel, 'A Flowing Culture: Images of Early Gujarati Indian-Islamic Migrants in Aotearoa New Zealand' (critical essay), *Transitions: Journal of Transient Migration* 1, no. 2 (1 June 2017): 253.

30. *FT*, 2 December 1925, 5, https://paperspast.natlib.govt.nz/newspapers/FRTIM19251202.2.28

31. Ibid.

32. Ibid., 4, https://paperspast.natlib.govt.nz/newspapers/FRTIM19260719.2.7

33. 'Our Visitors,' *FT*, 19 July 1926, 4.

34. Labour Department — Immigration, 'Policy documents and files relating to Indians,' 22/1/134 (33/156M), 2 March 1955.

35. Labour Department 22/1/134, 6 July 1961.

36. Ibid., 29 September 1962.

37. See, Leckie, *Indian Settlers*, 115–16.

38. Mandrika Rupa, *Taamara/Sangam* (Auckland: Maori Television), 27 October 2004.

39. McLeod, *Punjabis in New Zealand*, 139.

40. Leckie, 'A Long Diaspora', 5–8.

41. *Sun*, 12 June 1929, 1; *Sun*, 17 June 1929.

42. Cited in Barbara Brookes, 'Gender, Work and Fears of a "Hybrid Race" in 1920s New Zealand,' *Gender and History* 19, no. 3 (2007): 507–08.

43. Ibid.

44. *Census of New Zealand*, 1926–36.

45. *NZPD* (240) 10 November 1934, 1181–82.

46. Brookes, 'Gender, Work,' 513.

Chapter seven. Contemporary Exclusion

1. When Sharma took his parliamentary oath in Sanskrit it sparked criticism from some Kiwi-Indian activists who were opposed to the growth of Hindutva. Journalist Michael Field asserted on social media that Sanskrit is a language of 'religious oppression and caste superiority'. Sandeep Singh in the *Indian Weekender* responded with 'NZ Journo's Charge Against Sanskrit Language and Kiwi-Parliamentarian Loaded with Ignorance and Bigotry,' *IW*, 25 November 2020, https://www.indianweekender.co.nz/Pages/ArticleDetails/7/14018/New-Zealand/NZ-journos-charge-against-Sanskrit-language-and-Kiwi-parliamentarian-loaded-wit. This heated exchange reminds us that there is no consensus among Kiwi-Indians today about a homogeneous collective identity, but, as I stress, this book focuses on discrimination against Kiwi-Indians, and not within the diaspora.
2. See, for example, Geoff Watson and the NZISA Historic Book Committee, *Sporting Foundations of New Zealand Indians: A Fifty Year History of the New Zealand Indian Sports Association* (Wellington: New Zealand Indian Sports Association, 2012).
3. See, for example, Alison Booth, 'Negotiating Indianness. Auckland's Shifting Cultural Festivities,' in Sekhar Bandyopadhyay and Jane Buckingham, eds., *Indians and the Antipodes: Networks, Boundaries, and Circulation* (New Delhi: Oxford University Press, 2018), 278–303.
4. See, for example, Janet McAllister, 'Passages from India,' *Metro* (NZ) (November 2002): 66–84; Leckie, *Indian Settlers*, 169–78.
5. Phil Gendall, Paul Spoonley and Andrew Butcher, *New Zealanders' Perceptions of Asia and Asian Peoples 1997–2011* (Wellington: Asia New Zealand Foundation, 2011).
6. Paul Rishworth, 'Human Rights — Freedom from Discrimination,' *Te Ara — the Encyclopedia of New Zealand*, last modified 28 June 2016, http://www.TeAra.govt.nz/en/human-rights/page-3
7. Erich Kolig, *New Zealand's Muslims and Multiculturalism* (Leiden: Brill, 2010), 10.
8. Stephanie Dobson, 'Asian Muslim Women Negotiating Identity in New Zealand,' in Paola Voci and Jacqueline Leckie, eds., *Localizing Asia in Aotearoa* (Wellington: Dunmore Publishing, 2011), 187–203.
9. Kirsty Johnston, 'Inside NZ's Alt-right,' *NZH*, 12 July 2017.
10. 'Explosion in Racial Attack at Home of Indian Family,' *Dominion*, 5 November 1997, 3.
11. Marin Kay and Joanne Black, 'A Tale Of Two Immigrants,' *Dominion Post*, 14 September 2002.
12. *NZPD*, 28 August 2002.
13. Ibid.
14. Audrey Young, 'Anti-racism Protester in Ugly Clash with Peters,' *NZH*, 4 September 2002, https://www.nzherald.co.nz/nz/news/article.cfm?c_id=1&objectid=2352705
15. Pat Booth and Yvonne Martin, 'The Inv-Asian,' *Eastern Courier*, 16 April 1993, 6–7; Deborah Coddington, 'Asian Angst: Is It Time to Send Some Back?,' *North & South*, December 2006, 38–47; Andrew Butcher and Paul Spoonley, 'Inv-Asian: Print Media Constructions of Asians and Asian Immigration,' in Voci and Leckie, *Localizing Asia in Aotearoa*, 98–115.
16. Butcher and Spoonley, 'Inv-Asian,' 104; Paul Spoonley and Andrew Trlin, *Making Sense of Multicultural New Zealand* (Palmerston North: New Settlers Programme, Massey University, 2004), summarise this research. See also Andrew Butcher, Paul Spoonley and Andrew Trlin, *Being Accepted: The Experience of Discrimination and Social Exclusion by Immigrants and Refugees in New Zealand* (Auckland: New Settlers Programme, Massey University, 2006).
17. CERD (Committee on the Elimination of Racial Discrimination), 82nd Session (March 2013): Consideration of reports, comments and information submitted by states parties under article 9 of the convention, http:// www2.ohchr.org/english/bodies/cerd/docs/co/CERD-C-NZL-CO-18-20_en.pdf
18. Nicola Legat, 'Murder Continued,' *Metro*, October 1994, 62–76; TV3, 'Under the Carpet.'
19. 'Holtz Guilty of Shiu Prasad's Murder,' *NZH*, 12 March 2002, https://www.nzherald.co.nz/nz/news/article.cfm?c_id=1&objectid=1191248
20. Ranjit Singh, 'Daylight Murder Angers Aucklanders,' *Indian Newslink*, 1 February 2008.

21. Alanah Eriksen, 'Krishna Murder Accused Appears in Court,' *NZH*, 29 January 2008, https://www.nzherald.co.nz/nz/news/article.cfm?c_id=1&objectid=10489308
22. Cate Brett, 'Sushila's Dairy,' *Press*, 19 August 2000. See also, 'Man Holds Up Dairy for Cigarettes,' *Press*, 15 December 1997, 7; Sinead O'Hanlon, 'Feisty Owner Combats Robbers,' *Press*, 6 October 1998, 2.
23. Legat, 'Murder Continued,'; TV3, 'Under the Carpet.'
24. Jam TV, 'The Changing Face of the New Zealand Dairy' (Prime Television, 2019).
25. David Fisher, 'Greatest NZ Stories: Life Rebuilt After Father's Murder but Pain Lingers,' *NZH*, 12 November 2013, https://www.nzherald.co.nz/nz/greatest-nz-stories-life-rebuilt-after-fathers-murder-but-pain-lingers/5FS66WKHKYEUKOMDRWW42HJ5PQ/
26. Kathryn Powley, *Herald on Sunday*, 4 August 2013.
27. George Heagney and Maxine Jacobs, 'Dairy Owners Fearful After String of Robberies; Demands Higher Police Presence at Stores,' *Stuff*, 19 August 2020, https://www.stuff.co.nz/national/crime/300084930/dairy-owners-fearful-after-string-of-robberies-demands-higher-police-presence-at-stores
28. Philip Kitchin, 'Police Look at Gang Links in Bashing of Immigrants,' *Dominion*, 29 March 2000, 10.
29. According to TV3, 'Under the Carpet.'
30. 'Explosion in Racial Attack at Home of Indian Family,' *Dominion*, 5 November 1997, 3.
31. *Dominion Post*, 6 August 2010, cited in Human Rights Commission, 'It Happened Here. Reports of Race and Religious Hate Crime in New Zealand 2004–2012' (Wellington), June 2019, https://www.hrc.co.nz/files/1515/6047/9685/It_Happened_Here_Reports_of_race_and_religious_hate_crime_in_New_Zealand_2004-2012.pdf. Other incidents of racially motivated physical and verbal abuse against Indians in Aotearoa are listed in this document.
32. Scott Hamilton, 'New Zealand's Long and Violent History of Anti-Indian Racism,' *Spinoff*, 27 June 2019, https://thespinoff.co.nz/atea/27-06-2019/prehistory-of-a-beating-new-zealands-violent-anti-indian-past/
33. Anna Leask, 'Racial Attack: Kiwi Beaten, Verbally Abused in Daylight Assault in Auckland's Sandringham,' *NZH*, 27 June 2019.
34. 'Girl Suffers Racial Abuse at Dunedin Park,' *ODT*, 15 January 2020.
35. Martin Kay, 'Racist Remarks About Immigrants "Common",' *Dominion Post*, 21 April 2004, A4.
36. Todd Nachowitz, 'Towards a Framework of Deep Diversity: Identity and Invisibility in the Indian Diaspora in New Zealand,' (PhD thesis, University of Waikato, 2015), https://hdl.handle.net/10289/9442. The survey was conducted online and did not represent a random sample.
37. Brittany Keogh, 'Meet the Bhikoo-Patels: Proud Kiwi Muslims for More than a Century,' *Stuff*, 24 March 2019, https://www.stuff.co.nz/national/christchurch-shooting/111388696/meet-the-bhikoopatels-five-generations-of-proud-kiwi-muslims
38. Leckie, Jacqueline, '"A Rich Tapestry": The Life and Heritage of Sir Anand Satyanand', in Bandyopadhyay and Buckingham, *Indians and the Antipodes*, 223–53.
39. Martin Kay, 'Henry Apology for G-G Race Comments', *Stuff*, 24 October 2010, http://www.stuff.co.nz/entertainment/tv/4194441/Henry-apology-for-G-G-race-comments
40. *Southland Times*, 3 March 2009, Cited in Human Rights Commission, 'It Happened Here'.
41. Sandeep Singh, 'Kiwi-Indian Sikh Subjected to Racist Slur in South Auckland — "Go Back to Your Country",' *IW*, 27 February 2017, https://www.indianweekender.co.nz/Pages/ArticleDetails/7/7665/New-Zealand/Kiwi-Indian-Sikh-subjected-to-racist-slur-in-South-Auckland-Go-back-to-your-cou
42. 'Racist Abuse: Victim Narindervir Singh Calls for Public Apology to the Punjabi Community,' *NZH*, 9 March 2017.
43. Ben Leahy and Charlotte Carter, '"Go Back to Your Country" — Kiwis Share Racism Stories,' *NZH*, 17 June 2018.
44. Corazon Miller, *NZH*, 5 December 2016.
45. Samantha Olley, '"No Indians": Rotorua, Christchurch Flat Ads "Racist",' *ODT*, 20 September 2019.
46. Rizwan Mohammad, 'Indian Tenants

Denied Rental Property Because "Indians Are Dirty",' *IW*, 16 May 2019, https://www.indianweekender.co.nz/Pages/ArticleDetails/7/10650/New-Zealand/Indian-tenants-denied-rental-property-because-Indians-are-dirty

47. *NZH*, 9 July 2003.

48. Lincoln Tan, 'Racism Blamed for Bar Ban,' *NZH*, 3 January 2014.

49. 'Wellington Bar Labels Indian Patrons as Rapists,' *IW*, 13 January 2014, https://www.indianweekender.co.nz/Pages/ArticleDetails/7/4153/New-Zealand/Wellington-bar-labels-Indian-patrons-as-rapists

50. Hannah Norton, 'Turbans Off Says Club,' *Manukau Courier*, 11 December 2009, http://www.stuff.co.nz/auckland/local-news/manukau-courier/3149116/Turbans-off-says-club

51. Brian Rudman, 'Intolerant Social Club Stuck in Racist Past,' *NZH*, 16 June 2010.

52. Lincoln Tan, 'Sikh Barred from Cossie Club over Turban,' *NZH*, 18 June 2015; 'Sikh Man Turned Away from Manurewa Cosmopolitan Club because He Was Wearing a Turban', *One News*, Breakfast, 9 December 2019, https://www.tvnz.co.nz/one-news/new-zealand/sikh-man-turned-away-manurewa-cosmopolitan-club-because-he-wearing-turban

53. Kay, 'Racist Remarks about Immigrants "Common"; Pio, *Sari: Indian Women at Work in New Zealand*, 68–86, discusses discrimination faced by Indian women in contemporary Aotearoa; Bridget Daldy, Jacques Poot and Matthew Roskruge, in 'Perception of Workplace Discrimination Among Immigrants and Native Born New Zealanders,' *Australian Journal of Labour Economics* 16, no. 1 (2013): 137–54, found that the highest likelihood of self-reported workplace discrimination was among migrants from Asia and the Pacific Islands. Discrimination is more likely to be reported by those with a higher education and at mid-career. See also Butcher, Spoonley and Trlin, *Being Accepted*, 17–28.

54. Khan, 'A Study of Fiji Indian Migrants In New Zealand'.

55. Joanna Lewin et al., 'Namasté New Zealand: Indian Employers and Employees in Auckland' (North Shore City: Integration of Immigrants Programme, Massey University, 2011), http://integrationofimmigrants.massey.ac.nz/publications_pdfs/Namaste%20New%20Zealand.pdf

56. Nachowitz, 'Towards a Framework of Deep Diversity', 2015.

57. Collins and Stringer, 'Temporary Migrant Worker Exploitation In New Zealand,' 52, also found that men born in India experienced high rates of discrimination.

58. *AS*, 1 June 1983.

59. *NZH*, 26 August 1983.

60. Kirsty Lawrence, 'Racist Backlash on the Campaign Trail,' *Waikato Times*, 23 June 2020.

61. Ibid.

62. Lincoln Tan, 'Indian Association Demands Apology from Simon Bridges for "Indian vs Chinese" Comments.' *NZH*, 19 October 2018, https://www.nzherald.co.nz/nz/news/article.cfm?c_id=1&objectid=12145092

63. Sandeep Singh, 'Partnership Visa: It's Time to Clear Dirt Around Kiwi-Indian Community,' *IW*, 7 November 2019, https://www.indianweekender.co.nz/Pages/ArticleDetails/7/11302/New-Zealand/Partnership-visa-Its-time-to-clear-dirt-around-Kiwi-Indian-community

64. Dev Nadkarni, 'Unwelcome Verbal Fireworks Mar Diwali,' *IW*, 1 November 2019, https://www.indianweekender.co.nz/Pages/ArticleDetails/52/11284/Editorials/Unwelcome-verbal-fireworks-mar-Diwali; Zane Small, '"Bollywood Overreaction": Shane Jones Digs in After Angering Indian Community, *IW*, 5 November 2019, https://www.newshub.co.nz/home/politics/2019/11/that-s-a-bollywood-overreaction-shane-jones-digs-in-after-angering-indian-community.html

65. Mark Quinlivan, 'Hannah Tamaki's Vision NZ Says It Will ban the Construction of Mosques, Temples and Other "Foreign Buildings",' *Newshub*, 11 November 2019, https://www.newshub.co.nz/home/politics/2019/11/hannah-tamaki-s-vision-nz-says-it-will-ban-the-construction-of-mosques-temples-and-other-foreign-buildings.html

66. Dan Satherley, 'Shane Jones Says Indian Students Have "Ruined" NZ Academic Institutions,' *Newshub*, 29 February 2020,https://www.newshub.co.nz/home/politics/2020/02/shane-jones-says-indian-students-have-ruined-nz-academic-institutions.

67. Sandeep Singh, 'Winston Peters' Defence of Shane Jones' Racist Comments Reflects Sickening "Victim-Blaming" Mindset' *IW*, 4 March 2020,

https://www.indianweekender.co.nz/Pages/ArticleDetails/7/11710/New-Zealand/Winston-Peters-defence-of-Shane-Jones-racist-comments-reflects-sickening-victim?fbclid=IwARouVUVXLLpaowqRytssyYHNAATFKe2-qZMWB_KMRDczVBudZoGgIhEIylg

68. Lizzie Marvelly, 'Sit Down Shane — You're Out of Tune,' *Weekend Herald*, 7 March 2020.

69. Lee and Cain, 'Diversity Dividends and the Dehumanisation of Immigrants', 201. See, for example, their discussion of Rachel Smalley, 'Indian Students Need to Go', *NZH*, 16 February 2017, http://www.nzherald.co.nz/nz/news/article.cfm?c_id=1&objectid=11801673

70. Nair, 'Of Racism and Coronavirus.'

71. HRC, 'NZ Human Rights,' 3 March 2020, https://www.hrc.co.nz/news/race-relations-commissioner-condemns-shane-jones-comments-against-indian-communities-racist-ignorant-and-harmful

72. Ireland Hendry-Tennent, 'Korean, Indian Community Groups Call for Hamish Walker to Apologise for "Racist" Comments,' *Newshub*, 10 July 2020, https://www.newshub.co.nz/home/politics/2020/07/korean-indian-community-groups-call-for-hamish-walker-to-apologise-for-racist-comments.html. Walker also passed confidential Covid-19 patient details to the media. He subsequently resigned from political office.

73. Ibid.

74. Melissa Chan-Green, 'Anti-racism Campaign Launched after Spike in Racial Attacks towards Asian Community,' *Newshub*, 13 July 2020, https://www.newshub.co.nz/home/new-zealand/2020/07/anti-racism-campaign-launched-after-spike-in-racial-attacks-towards-asian-community.html

75. HRC, 'Meng Foon: Covid-19 Coronavirus Fear No Excuse for Racism,' 11 May 2020, https://covid19.hrc.co.nz/meng_foon_covid_19_coronavirus_fear_no_excuse_for_racism

76. Nair, 'Of Racism and Coronavirus.'

77. 'Explosion in Racial Attack at Home of Indian Family,' *Dominion*, 5 November 1997, 3; 'Racism's Ugly Face,' *Nelson Mail*, 6 November 1997.

78. Human Rights Commission, 'Taika's Challenge to Kiwis to Give Nothing to Racism,' 17 November 2017, https://www.hrc.co.nz/news/taikas-challenge-kiwis-give-nothing-racism-takes-out-top-honours/

79. Olley, 'No Indians.'

80. Chan-Green, 'Anti-racism Campaign.'

81. Ibid.

82. 'Wellington Train Conductor Stops and Demands a Racist Passenger to Get Off,' *NZH*, 10 August 2019.

83. Paul Williams, 'Foxton Chef Peppered by Racist Spray', *Horowhenua Chronicle*, 7 August 2019.

84. Carolyne Meng-Yee, 'This Is Who We Are', *NZH*, 25 March 2019.

Bibliography

A note on archives

Several archival sources detailed in the endnotes are from former government departments (Customs, Internal Affairs, Justice, Labour — Immigration Division, Legislative, Māori Affairs), and were consulted at either National Archives, Wellington, or in government departments when I was researching my PhD thesis during 1977–81. Permission was given to publish these sources. Further details of these archives can be found in Jacqueline Leckie, 'They Sleep Standing Up: Gujaratis in New Zealand to 1945' (PhD thesis, University of Otago, Dunedin, 1981), 681–84. Available at http://hdl.handle.net/10523/9118

By 2021, several records that were formerly held in government departments had been transferred to Archives New Zealand Te Rua Mahara o te Kāwanatanga, Wellington, where the records may be listed under a new code.

Other unpublished primary sources

- India Office Library records
- British Museum records
- Indian Central Association (Inc.), Annual Conference, Report and Financial Statements, 1952–70.
- Jelal Natali, newspaper cuttings (cited as memorabilia)
- George Parvin, secretary of the White New Zealand League, newspaper cuttings
- Wellington City Council and City Engineer's Department, 1918, minutes
- Various unpublished documents provided to me by members of the Indian community when I was compiling *Indian Settlers: The Story of a New Zealand South Asian Community*. (Dunedin: Otago University Press, 2007)

Newspapers and other media sources

Most newspapers below are available online until 1945 at Papers Past, National Library of New Zealand Te Puna Mātauranga o Aotearoa, https://paperspast.natlib.govt.nz/newspapers

- *Ashburton Guardian*, 1923
- *Auckland Star*, 1918–83
- *Bay of Plenty Beacon*, 1945
- *Dominion*, 1913; 1997–2000
- *Dominion Post*, 2002–10
- *Evening News*, 2000
- *Evening Post*, 1920–40
- *Franklin County News*, 1986
- *Franklin Times*, 1925–52
- *Gisborne Herald*, 1942
- *Hawke's Bay Today*, 2012
- *Herald on Sunday*, 2013
- *Horowhenua Chronicle*, 2019
- *Indian Newslink*, 2008

- *Indian Weekender*, 2013–20
- *Lyttelton Times*, 1908
- *Manawatu Standard*, 1907–8
- *Manukau Courier*, 2009
- *Maoriland Worker*, 1920
- *Nelson Mail*, 1997
- *New Zealand Herald*, 1920–2019
- *New Zealand Observer*, 1937
- *New Zealand Times*, 1907
- *Newshub*, 2020
- *NZ Truth*, 1909, 1912
- *One News*, 2019
- *Otago Daily Times*, 1875; 1942; 1990–2020
- *Otago Witness*, 1885–1907
- *Quick March*, 1920
- *Southland Times*, 2009
- *Stuff*, 2010; 2019–20
- *The Sun* (Christchurch), 1915; 1929
- *The Press*, 1920; 1997–2000
- *The Times*, 1895
- *Waikato Times*, 1920; 1960; 2020
- *Wairarapa Daily Times*, 1921
- *Weekend Herald*, 2020

Publications

Andrews, Robyn. 'Did You Know Your Great Grandmother Was an Indian Princess? Early Anglo Indian Arrivals in New Zealand.' In *Indians and the Antipodes: Networks, Boundaries, and Circulation*, edited by Sekhar Bandyopadhyay and Jane Buckingham, 210–232. New Delhi: Oxford University Press, 2018.

Appendix to the Journal of the House of Representatives, 1929, 1946–47. Available at https://paperspast.natlib.govt.nz/parliamentary/appendix-to-the-journals-of-the-house-of-representatives

Ansell, Amy Elizabeth. *Race and Ethnicity: The Key Concepts*. Abingdon, UK: Routledge, 2013.

Atkinson, David C. *The Burden of White Supremacy: Containing Asian Migration in the British Empire and the United States*. Chapel Hill: University of North Carolina Press, 2016.

Bandyopadhyay, Sekhar. 'Reinventing Indian Identity In Multicultural New Zealand.' In *Asia in the Making of New Zealand*, edited by Henry Johnson and Brian Moloughney, 125–46. Auckland: Auckland University Press, 2006.

——— 'A History of Small Numbers: Indians in New Zealand, 1890–1930.' *New Zealand Journal of History* 43, no. 2 (October 2009): 150–68.

Bartholomew, Robert E. *No Maori Allowed: New Zealand's Forgotten History of Racial Segregation: How a Generation of Māori Children Perished in the Fields of Pukekohe*. Auckland: Robert E. Bartholomew, 2020.

Beaglehole, Ann. *Refuge New Zealand: A Nation's Response to Refugees and Asylum Seekers*. Dunedin: Otago University Press, 2013.

——— 'Immigration Regulation — 1946–1985: Gradual Change.' *Te Ara — the Encyclopedia of New Zealand*, published 8 February 2005, updated 18 August 2015, 4–5. http://www.TeAra.govt.nz/en/immigration-regulation/pages-4-5

Belich, James. *Paradise Reforged: A History of the New Zealanders from the 1880s to the Year 2000*. Auckland: Allen Lane: Penguin Press, 2001.

Bhana, Surendra, and Bridglal Pachai, eds. *A Documentary History of Indian South Africans*. Cape Town: New Africa Books, 1984.

Booth, Alison. 'Negotiating Indianness: Auckland's Shifting Cultural Festivities.' In *Indians and the Antipodes: Networks, Boundaries, and Circulation*, edited by Sekhar Bandyopadhyay and Jane Buckingham, 278–303. New Delhi: Oxford University Press, 2018.

Booth, Pat, and Yvonne Martin. 'The Inv-Asian.' *Eastern Courier*, 16 April 1993, 6–7.

Brawley, Sean. 'No "White Policy" in New Zealand: Fact and Fiction in New Zealand's Asian Immigration Record, 1946–1978.' *New Zealand Journal of History* 27, no. 1 (1993): 16–36.

Brookes, Barbara. 'Gender, Work and Fears of a "Hybrid Race" in 1920s New Zealand.' *Gender and History* 19, no. 3 (2007): 501–18.

Butcher, Andrew. '"They Do Not Lead Sanitary Lives": New Zealanders' Perceptions of India and Indians in 2010.' *Communication Journal of New Zealand* 12 (2011): 8–27.

——— 'Immigrants of Doubtful Value: Translating Policy Discourse About International Students in New Zealand.' In *Migration, Education and Translation: Cross-Disciplinary Perspectives on Human Mobility and Cultural Encounters in Education Settings*, edited by Vivienne Anderson and Henry Johnson, 117–28. Abingdon, UK: Routledge, 2020.

——— and Paul Spoonley. 'Inv-Asian: Print Media Constructions of Asians and Asian Immigration.' In *Localizing Asia in Aotearoa*, edited by Paola Voci and Jacqueline Leckie, 98–115. Wellington: Dunmore Publishing, 2011.

———, Paul Spoonley, and Andrew Trlin. *Being Accepted: The Experience of Discrimination and Social Exclusion by Immigrants and Refugees in New Zealand*. Auckland: New Settlers Programme, Massey University, 2006.

Byrnes, Giselle. *The New Oxford History of New Zealand*. Melbourne: Oxford University Press, 2009.

——— and Catharine Coleborne, 'Editorial Introduction: The Utility and Futility of "The Nation" in Histories of Aotearoa New Zealand.' *New Zealand Journal of History* 45, no. 1 (April 2011): 1–14.

CERD. Committee on the Elimination of Racial Discrimination: 82nd Session: Consideration of reports, comments and information submitted by states parties under article 9 of the convention. March 2013. http:// www2.ohchr.org/english/bodies/cerd/docs/co/CERD-C-NZL-CO-18-20_en.pdf

Chibba, Uka. *Indians in Pukekohe 1918–2006*. Pukekohe: Private publication, 2007.

Coddington, Deborah. 'Asian Angst. Is it Time to Send Some Back?', *North & South*, December 2006: 38–47.

Collins, Francis, and Christina Stringer, 'Temporary Migrant Worker Exploitation in New Zealand,' July 2019. Report to MBIE, https://www.mbie.govt.nz/dmsdocument/7109-temporary-migrant-worker-exploitation-in-new-zealand

Daji, Bhanu. 'Ganga Ravji.' In *With a Suitcase of Saris: From India to Aotearoa: Stories of Pioneer Indian Women*, edited by Rebecca Lal and compiled by Vasanti Unka, 34–39. Auckland: Aditi Indian Women's Collective, My Sunroom, 2016.

Daldy, Bridget, Jacques Poot and Matthew Roskruge. 'Perception of Workplace Discrimination Among Immigrants and Native Born New Zealanders.' *Australian Journal of Labour Economics* 16, no. 1 (2013): 137–154.

Dobson, Stephanie. 'Asian Muslim Women Negotiating Identity in New Zealand.' In *Localizing*

Asia in Aotearoa, edited by Paola Voci and Jacqueline Leckie, 187–203. Wellington: Dunmore Publishing, 2011.

Drury, Abdullah. 'Don't Panic: Muslims in the Waikato Region of New Zealand.' *Waikato Islamic Studies Review* 2, no. 10 (2016): 40–61.

——— 'Once Were Mahometans: Muslims in the South Island of New Zealand, Mid-19th to Late 20th Century, with Special Reference to Canterbury.' MPhil thesis, University of Waikato, 2016. https://hdl.handle.net/10289/10630

——— 'Mahometans on the Edge of Colonial Empire: Antipodean Experiences.' *Islam and Christian–Muslim Relations* 29, no. 1 (2018): 71–87.

Du Bois, W. E. B. *The Souls of Black Folk*. New York: New American Library, 1903.

Entwistle, Peter. *Taka: A Vignette Life of William Tucker 1784–1817: Convict, Sealer, Trader in Human Heads, Otago Settler, New Zealand's First Art Dealer*. Dunedin: Port Daniel Press, 2005.

Gendall, Phil, Paul Spoonley and Andrew Butcher. *New Zealanders' Perceptions of Asia and Asian Peoples 1997–2011*. Wellington: Asia New Zealand Foundation, 2011.

Ghosh, Gautam, and Jacqueline Leckie, eds. *Asians and the New Multiculturalism in Aotearoa New Zealand*. Dunedin: Otago University Press, 2015.

Gregory, J. W. *The Menace of Colour*. London: Seeley, Service & Co, 1925. https://wellcome collection.org/works/ea2739jv/items?langCode=eng&sierraId=b29815095&canvas=7

Hamilton, Scott. 'New Zealand's Long and Violent History of Anti-Indian Racism.' *The Spinoff*, 27 June 2019. https://thespinoff.co.nz/atea/27-06-2019/prehistory-of-a-beating-new-zealands-violent-anti-indian-past/

Harris, Marvin. *Patterns of Race in the Americas*. Westport, CT: Greenwood Press, 1980.

Howard, Basil. *Rakiura: A History of Stewart Island, New Zealand*. Dunedin: A. H. & A. W. Reed, 1974 [1940].

Human Rights Commission. 'It Happened Here. Reports of Race and Religious Hate Crime in New Zealand 2004–2012.' Wellington, June 2019. https://www.hrc.co.nz/files/1515/6047/9685/It_Happened_Here_Reports_of_race_and_religious_hate_crime_in_New_Zealand_2004-2012.pdf

Huttenback, Robert A. *Racism and Empire: White Settlers and Colored Immigrants in the British Self-Governing Colonies, 1830–1910*. Ithaca, NY: Cornell University Press, 1976.

Ip, Manying. 'Chinese Immigration to Australia and New Zealand: Government Policies and Race Relations.' In *Routledge Handbook of the Chinese Diaspora*, edited by T. Chee-Beng, 156–175. Abingdon, UK: Routledge, 2013.

——— and Jacqueline Leckie. '"Chinamen" and "Hindoos"': Beyond Stereotypes to Kiwi Asians.' In *Localizing Asia in Aotearoa*, edited by Paola Voci and Jacqueline Leckie, 77–106. Wellington: Dunmore Publishing, 2011.

Jackson, Moana. 'The Connection Between White Supremacy and Colonisation.' *E-Tāngata*, 24 March 2019. https://e-tangata.co.nz/comment- and-analysis/the-connection-between-white-supremacy/

Johnson, Ella. 'Soldier Singh, an Indian ANZAC.' Auckland War Memorial Museum Tāmaki Paenga Hira, 2017. www.aucklandmuseum.com/war-memorial/online-cenotaph/features/soldier-singh-an-indian-anzac

Kenna, Len, and Crystal Jordan. 'Ratan Chand Mehra, an Anzac.' 25 April 2015. http://australianindianhistory.com/ratan-chand-mehra-an-anzac/

——— 'Sham Singh New Zealand Army WWI.' 25 April 2015. http://australianindianhistory.com/sham-singh-an-anzac/

Kernot, Bernie. *People of the Four Winds.* Wellington: Hicks, Smith & Sons, 1972.

Khan, Robert L. 'A Study of Fiji Indian Migrants In New Zealand: Their Migration and Settlement Management and Experiences.' PhD thesis, Massey University, 2011. http://hdl.handle.net/10179/2993

King, Michael. *The Penguin History of New Zealand.* Auckland: Penguin, 2003.

Kolig, Erich. *New Zealand's Muslims and Multiculturalism.* Leiden: Brill, 2010.

Lake, Marilyn, and Henry Reynolds. *Drawing the Global Colour Line: White Men's Countries and the International Challenge of Racial Equality.* Carlton: Melbourne University Publishing, 2008.

Lal, Brij V., Peter Reeves and Rajesh Rai, eds. *The Encyclopedia of the Indian Diaspora.* Singapore: Éditions Didier Millet/National University of Singapore, 2006.

Leckie, Jacqueline. 'They Sleep Standing Up: Gujaratis in New Zealand to 1945.' PhD thesis, Dunedin, University of Otago, 1981. http://hdl.handle.net/10523/9118

——— 'In Defence of Race and Empire: The White New Zealand League at Pukekohe.' *The New Zealand Journal of History* 19, no. 2 (1985): 103–29.

——— 'Natali, Jelal Kalyanji.' *Dictionary of New Zealand Biography, Te Ara — the Encyclopedia of New Zealand*, first published in 2000. https://teara.govt.nz/en/biographies/5n1/natali-jelal-kalyanji (accessed 2 January 2021).

——— 'Fijians,' *Te Ara — the Encyclopedia of New Zealand*, first published in 2005, updated 25 March 2015. http://www.TeAra.govt.nz/en/fijians (accessed 7 March 2020).

——— *Indian Settlers: The Story of a New Zealand South Asian Community*. Dunedin: Otago University Press, 2007.

——— 'A Long Diaspora: Indian Settlement in Aotearoa/New Zealand.' In *India in New Zealand: Local Identities, Global Relations*, edited by Sekhar Bandyopadhyay, 45–63. Dunedin: Otago University Press, 2010.

——— 'Indians in the South Pacific: Recentred Disaporas.' In *Recentring Asia: Histories, Encounters, Identities,* edited by Jacob Edmond, Henry Johnson and Jacqueline Leckie, 54–84. Leiden: Global Oriental/Brill, 2011.

——— 'A Rich Tapestry': The Life and Heritage of Sir Anand Satyanand.' In *India and the Antipodes: Networks, Boundaries, and Circulation*, edited by Sekhar Bandyopadhyay and Jane Buckingham, 223–53. New Delhi: Oxford University Press, 2018.

Lee, Erika. 'The "Yellow Peril" and Asian Exclusion in the Americas.' *Pacific Historical Review* 76 (2007): 537–62.

Lee, Sandy, and Trudie Cain. 'Diversity Dividends and the Dehumanisation of Immigrants in the News Media in Aotearoa New Zealand.' *New Zealand Population Review* 45 (2019): 185–210.

Legat, Nicola. 'Murder Continued.' *Metro* (NZ), October 1994: 62–76.

Lewin, Joanna, Carina Meares, Trudie Cain, Paul Spoonley, Robin Peace and Elsie Ho. 'Namasté New Zealand: Indian Employers and Employees in Auckland.' North Shore City: Integration of Immigrants Programme, Massey University, 2011. http://integrationofimmigrants.massey.ac.nz/publications_pdfs/Namaste%20New%20Zealand.pdf

Lochore, R. A. *From Europe to New Zealand: An Account of Our Continental European Settlers.* Wellington: A.H. & A.W. Reed, with the New Zealand Institute of International Affairs, 1951.

Matthewman, Steve. 'Pākehā Ethnicity. The Politics of White Privilege.' In *A Land of Milk and Honey? Making Sense of Aotearoa New Zealand*, edited by Avril Bell, Vivienne Elizabeth, Tracey McIntosh and Matt Wynyard, 60–67. Auckland: Auckland University Press, 2018.

Mcallister, Janet. 'Passages from India.' *Metro* (NZ), November 2002, 66–84.

McCabe, Jane. '"An Ideal Life": Anglo-Indians in the New Zealand Expeditionary Force.' In *Endurance and the First World War: Experiences and Legacies in New Zealand and Australia*, edited by David Monger, Katie Pickles and Sarah Murray, 196–214. Newcastle: Cambridge Scholars Publishing, 2014.

——— *Kalimpong Kids: The New Zealand Story, in Pictures*. Dunedin: Otago University Press, 2020.

McKeown, Adam. *Melancholy Order: Asian Migration and the Globalization of Borders*. New York, NY: Columbia University Press, 2008.

McLeod, W. H. *A List of Punjabi Immigrants in New Zealand 1890–1939*. Hamilton: Central Indian Association Country Section, 1984.

——— *Punjabis in New Zealand: A History of Punjabi Migration 1890–1940*. Amritsar: Guru Nanak Dev University, 1986.

——— and S. S. Bhullar. *Punjab to Aotearoa: Migration and Settlement of Punjabis in New Zealand, 1890–1990*. Hamilton: New Zealand Indian Association Country Section, 1992.

Munshi, Sherally. 'Immigration, Imperialism, and the Legacies of Indian Exclusion.' *Yale Journal of Law and the Humanities* 28, no. 1 (2015): 51–104. https://digitalcommons.law.yale.edu/yjlh/vol28/iss1/2

Murphy, Nigel. 'Report on Indian Community Grievances.' Commissioned by New Zealand Indian Central Association Grievances Committee, 2007.

——— '"Maoriland" and "Yellow Peril": Discourses of Maori and Chinese in the Formation of New Zealand's National Identity.' In *The Dragon and the Taniwha: Maori and Chinese in New Zealand*, edited by Manying Ip, 56–88. Auckland: Auckland University Press, 2009.

Nachowitz, Todd. 'Towards a Framework of Deep Diversity: Identity and Invisibility in the Indian Diaspora in New Zealand.' PhD thesis, University of Waikato, 2015. https://hdl.handle.net/10289/9442

——— 'Identity and Invisibility: Early Indian Presence in Aotearoa New Zealand, 1769–1850.' In *Indians and the Antipodes: Networks, Boundaries, and Circulation*, edited by Sekhar Bandyopadhyay and Jane Buckingham, 26–61. New Delhi: Oxford University Press, 2018.

Nairn, Angelique. 'What Is with All the Hate? A Thematic Analysis of New Zealanders' Attitudes to the Human Rights Commission's "Give Nothing to Racism" Social Marketing Campaign.' *New Zealand Sociology* 35, no. 1 (2020): 97–122.

Nakhid, Camille, and Heather Devere. 'Negotiating Multiculturalism and the Treaty of Waitangi.' In *Asians and the New Multiculturalism in Aotearoa New Zealand*, edited by Gautam Ghosh and Jacqueline Leckie, 61–89. Dunedin: Otago University Press, 2015.

New Zealand Parliamentary Debates. Wellington: Government Printer, 1895, 1913, 1920, 1934, 2002. Also known as *Hansard*. https://www.parliament.nz/en/pb/hansard-debates/historical-hansard/

New Zealand Political Reform League. *Handbook for Reform Party Candidates*. Wellington: Wright & Carman, 1914.

New Zealand Statutes. Wellington: Government Printer, 1920.

O'Connor, Peter S. 'Keeping New Zealand White, 1908–1920.' *New Zealand Journal of History* 2, no. 1 (1968): 41–65.

Olssen, Erik. 'Towards the Ideal Society.' In *The People and the Land / Te Tangata Me Te Whenua*, edited by Judith Binney, Judith Bassett and Erik Olssen, 235–252. Wellington: Bridget Williams Books, 2018.

Pack, Sylvia, Keith Tuffin and Antonia Lyons. 'Accounts of Blatant Racism against Māori in Aotearoa New Zealand.' *Sites. A Journal of Social Anthropology and Cultural Studies* 13, no. 2 (2016): 85–110.

Patel, Rafik. 'A Flowing Culture: Images of Early Gujarati Indian-Islamic Migrants in Aotearoa New Zealand'. *Transitions: Journal of Transient Migration* 1, no. 2 (1 June 2017): 251–67.

Paul, Diane B., John Stenhouse and Hamish G. Spencer. *Eugenics at the Edges of Empire New Zealand, Australia, Canada and South Africa*. Cham: Springer International Publishing, 2018.

Perkins, Jack. Interview with Mandrika Rupa, 'The Quarter Acre Indians.' *Spectrum*, 997 (Wellington: National Radio), 14 February 1998.

Pierce, Chester M., Jean V. Carew, Diane Pierce-Gonzalez and Deborah Wills. 'An Experiment in Racism: TV Commercials.' *Education and Urban Society* 10, no. 1 (November 1977): 61–87.

Pio, Edwina. *Sari: Indian Women at Work in New Zealand*. Wellington: Dunmore Publishing, 2008.

Prasad, Indra. 'Silent Discontent: Experiences of Everyday Racism in New Zealand = He Amuamu Nohopuku: He Whakapātanga Whakatoihara Tangata Ia Rā, Ia Rā, Ki Aotearoa.' MA thesis, Victoria University of Wellington, 2000.

Puk, James. 'Maori as Honorary Members of the White Tribe.' *The Journal of Imperial and Commonwealth History* 29, no. 3, (2001): 33–54.

Raj, Sushma. 'Australia. 1901 and After.' In *The Encyclopedia of the Indian Diaspora*, edited by Brij V. Lal, Peter Reeves and Rajesh Rai, 383–85. Singapore: Éditions Didier Millet/National University of Singapore, 2006.

Rishworth, Paul. 'Human Rights — Freedom from Discrimination.' *Te Ara — the Encyclopedia of New Zealand*, last modified 28 June 2016. http://www.TeAra.govt.nz/en/human-rights/page-3

Roche, Michael, and Sita Venkateswar. 'Neither Natural-born British Subjects nor Aliens.' In *Experience of a Lifetime: People, Personalities and Leaders in the First World War*, edited by John Crawford, David Littlewood and James Watson, 138–52. Auckland: Massey University Press, 2016.

——— 'Indian Migration to New Zealand in the 1920s. Deciphering the Immigration Restriction Amendment Act, 1920.' In *Indians and the Antipodes: Networks, Boundaries, and Circulation*, edited by Sekhar Bandyopadhyay and Jane Buckingham, 129–61. New Delhi: Oxford University Press, 2018.

Roy, W. T. 'Immigration Policy and Legislation.' In *Immigrants in New Zealand*, edited by Keith Westhead Thomson and Andrew Drago Trlin, 15–24. Palmerston North: Massey University, 1970.

Rupa, Mandrika, *Taamara/Sangam*. Auckland, Maori Television, 27 October 2004.

Salmond, Anne. *Between Worlds: Early Exchanges Between Maori and Europeans 1773–1815*. Auckland: Penguin, 1997.

Sastri, Srinivasa. 'Report by Right Honourable V. S. Srinivasa Sastri P. C. Regarding his Deputation to Dominions of Australia, New Zealand and Canada.' Simla: Central Government Press, 1923.

Sinclair, Keith. *A History of New Zealand*. Harmondsworth: Penguin, 1959.

——— 'Why Are Race Relations in New Zealand Better Than in South Africa, South Australia or South Dakota?' *The New Zealand Journal of History* 5, no. 2 (October 1971): 121–27.

Singh, Harpreet. 'From Guru Nanak to New Zealand: Mobility in the Sikh Tradition and the History of the Sikh Community in New Zealand to 1947.' PhD thesis, University of Otago, 2016. http://hdl.handle.net/10523/6810

Smith, Ian. *Pākehā Settlements in a Māori World New Zealand Archaeology, 1769–1860*. Wellington: Bridget Williams Books, 2020.

Spoonley, Paul. '"I Made a Space For You": Renegotiating National Identity and Citizenship in Contemporary Aotearoa New Zealand.' In *Asians and the New Multiculturalism in Aotearoa New Zealand,* edited by Gautam Ghosh and Jacqueline Leckie, 39–60. Dunedin: Otago University Press, 2015.

——— and Walter Hirsh. *Between the Lines: Racism and the New Zealand Media.* Auckland: Heinemann Reed, 1990.

——— and Andrew Trlin. *Making Sense of Multicultural New Zealand.* Palmerston North: New Settlers Programme, Massey University, 2004.

Stephan, Cookie White, and Walter G. Stephan. 'The Measurement of Racial and Ethnic Identity.' *International Journal of Intercultural Relations* 24, no. 5 (2000): 541–52.

Sue, Derald Wing. *Microaggressions in Everyday Life: Race, Gender, and Sexual Orientation.* Hoboken, NJ: Wiley, 2010.

———, Christina M. Capodilupo, Gina C. Torino, Jennifer M. Bucceri, Aisha M. B. Holder, Kevin L. Nadal and Marta Esquilin. 'Racial Microaggression in Everyday life: Implications for Clinical Practice.' *American Psychologist* 62, no. 4 (2007): 271–86.

Tinker, Hugh. 'Odd Man Out: The Loneliness of the Indian Colonial Politician — The Career of Manilal Doctor.' *Journal of Imperial and Commonwealth History* 2, no. 1 (1974): 226–43.

Tiwari, Kapil N. *Indians in New Zealand, Studies in a Sub Culture.* Wellington: Price Milburn for the New Zealand Indian Central Association, 1980.

Towie, Max. 'Deported and Destitute: Indian Students Say New Zealand Failed Them.' *The Spinoff*, 2 February 2019. https://thespinoff.co.nz/society/02-02-2019/deported-and-destitute-indian-students-say-new-zealand-failed-them/

'Under the Carpet.' TV3 documentary, *Inside New Zealand*, 31 June 1994.

Waikaremoana, Waitoki. '"This Is Not Us": But Actually, It Is. Talking About When to Raise the Issue of Colonisation.' *New Zealand Journal of Psychology (Online)* 48, no. 1 (2019): 140–45. https://hdl.handle.net/10289/12680

Watson, Geoff, and the NZISA Historic Book Committee. *Sporting Foundations of New Zealand Indians: A Fifty Year History of the New Zealand Indian Sports Association.* Wellington: New Zealand Indian Sports Association, 2012.

Wellington Indian Association Inc. *Golden Jubilee 1925–1926–1975–1976.* Wellington: 1976.

Wellington Indian Sports Club. *Wellington Indian Sports Club: The First 50 Years 1935–1985.* Wellington: Zodiac Printing, 1985.

White New Zealand League. 'Citizens of the Future Are the Children of Today.' Pukekohe: White New Zealand League, 1926 (Hocken Collections, Uare Taoka o Hākena, University of Otago).

——— 'Don't Fail to Read this Appeal.' Pukekohe: White New Zealand League, 1927 (Hocken Collections, Uare Taoka o Hākena, University of Otago).

Williams, Alan. *Edward Peters (Black Peter): The Discoverer of the First Workable Goldfield in Otago.* Balclutha: Clutha Print, 2009.

Williams, Jacqueline. 'A Study of the Gujarati Community in New Zealand Against the Background of Immigration Legislation to 1930.' BA (hons) dissertation, University of Otago, 1976.

Winder, Virginia. Singi Moral: A Fruitful Life.' Puke Ariki, created 24 March 2004, accessed 19 January 2021, https://terangiaoaonunui.pukeariki.com/all-stories/taranaki-stories/singi-moral-a-fruitful-life/

Image Credits

Every effort has been made to trace the copyright holders and obtain permission for the use of all images reproduced in this book. Copyright owners are invited to contact the publisher. The support and permission provided by various individuals, organisations and institutions are gratefully acknowledged.

19 Courtesy Craig Giddens

20 Alexander Turnbull Library, Ref: N-P-2189-28., *Otago Witness*, 5 December 1885, 28, https://paperspast.natlib.govt.nz/newspapers/OW18851205.2.123

21 Courtesy Jacqueline Leckie

23 *Free Lance*, 27 August 1947, 29

23 Alexander Turnbull Library, Ref: EP/1972/5327/5-F

25 Courtesy Country Section, NZICA

27 *New Zealand Herald*

30 *Illustrated Australian News*, 1 May 1893, http://handle.slv.vic.gov.au/10381/254932

30 Library and Archives Canada

33 Alexander Turnbull Library, Ref: N-P-2192-8., *Evening Post*, 14 January 1930, 8, https://paperspast.natlib.govt.nz/newspapers/EP19300114.2.57.4

40 Courtesy Harshadbhai Bhana

43 Courtesy Manisha Morar

45 Photograph by W. Beattie, Auckland Libraries Heritage Collections, AWNS-19140709-50-1

46 *NZ Truth*, 6 January 1912, 1, https://paperspast.natlib.govt.nz/newspapers/NZTR19120106.2.2

49 Archives New Zealand Te Rua Mahara o te Kāwanatanga, ACGV 8840, L28, R241881234, 1/1918

51 Cartoon by 'Slim', *New Zealand Observer*, 10 July 1920, 1, https://paperspast.natlib.govt.nz/newspapers/observer/1920/07/10/1

52 Alexander Turnbull Library, Ref: N-P-2190-7., *New Zealand Herald*, 26 May 1920, 7, https://paperspast.natlib.govt.nz/newspapers/NZH19200526.2.78

52 Cartoon by William Blomfield, *New Zealand Observer*, 29 May 1920, 15, https://paperspast.natlib.govt.nz/newspapers/TO19200529.2.24

54 Cartoon by Tom Ellis Glover, *Free Lance*, 1 December 1920, 3, https://paperspast.natlib.govt.nz/newspapers/NZFL19201201.2.4.1

57 Courtesy Bhanu Daji

60 Courtesy NZICA

61 Courtesy NZICA

63 Courtesy Madanjeet Bange

68 Courtesy Manisha Morar

69 Courtesy Manisha Morar

75 Cartoon by William Blomfield, *New Zealand Observer*, 26 April 1919, 13, https://paperspast.natlib.govt.nz/newspapers/TO19190426.2.23

76 Auckland Libraries Heritage Collections, 755-ALB18-39-1

78 Courtesy Veena Parsot

81 Hocken Collections, Uare Taoka o Hākena, University of Otago

81 Hocken Collections, Uare Taoka o Hākena, University of Otago

82 Hocken Collections, Uare Taoka o Hākena, University of Otago, Ref: Hoc 5/1/1

87 *Franklin Times*, 3 February 1926, 4, https://paperspast.natlib.govt.nz/newspapers/FRTIM19260203.2.12.2

87 *Franklin Times*, 21 June 1929, 4, https://paperspast.natlib.govt.nz/newspapers/FRTIM19290621.2.15.1

87 *Evening Post*, 24 September 1932, 14, https://paperspast.natlib.govt.nz/newspapers/EP19320924.2.121

91 *Auckland Star*, 8 June 1926, 15, https://paperspast.natlib.govt.nz/newspapers/AS19260608.2.160.10

91 *Auckland Star*, 6 January 1926, 9, https://paperspast.natlib.govt.nz/newspapers/AS19260106.2.106.5

91 *Auckland Star*, 17 April 1926, 16, https://paperspast.natlib.govt.nz/newspapers/AS19260417.2.168.7

93 Courtesy Country Section NZICA

94 Courtesy NZICA

97 Archives New Zealand Te Rua Mahara o te Kāwanatanga, "Miscellaneous - [Asian Immigration] 1916 – 1944," AAAC, 6015 Accession W4686, R337672, 13/a, 158/15

103 *Free Lance*, 7 July 1926, 33. Courtesy Auckland Institute and Museum

103 Wellington City Council Archives, 00158-466-b

106 Courtesy Wellington Indian Association

107 Alexander Turnbull Library, Ref: N-P-2193-8., *Evening Post*, 27 January 1932, 8, https://paperspast.natlib.govt.nz/newspapers/EP19320127.2.67

108 *Christchurch Star Sports*, 23 September 1967

111 Courtesy Hew McLeod; Country Section NZICA

111 Auckland Libraries Heritage Collections, NZG-19101130-31-1

112 *Free Lance*, 9 June 1920, 3, https://paperspast.natlib.govt.nz/newspapers/free-lance/1920/06/09/3

121 Courtesy Paul Patel

124 Courtesy Sumitra Dhanjee

130 Courtesy Craig Giddens

133 Alexander Turnbull Library, Ref: PAColl-0184-1-016

133 Archives New Zealand Te Rua Mahara o te Kāwanatanga, ACGV 8840, R24188098, L28/3, 10/1917

135 Archives New Zealand Te Rua Mahara o te Kāwanatanga, R7817714

139 Courtesy M.J. Mills family; Online Cenotaph, https://www.aucklandmuseum.com/war-memorial/online-cenotaph

141 *Franklin Times*, 9 December 1940, 3, https://paperspast.natlib.govt.nz/newspapers/FRTIM19401209.2.12

142 *Auckland Star*, 11 June 1940, 6, https://paperspast.natlib.govt.nz/newspapers/AS19400611.2.46.4

146 Courtesy Manisha Morar

155 Christchurch City Libraries, CCL-PhotoCD18-MG-0047

159 *New Zealand Observer*, 11 February 1937

160 *Bay of Plenty Beacon*, 16 November 1943, 4 https://paperspast.natlib.govt.nz/newspapers/BPB19431116.2.15.1

163 © Ans Westra AWM-01-08-F09

165 Courtesy Ramon Wallabh

166 *Auckland Star*, 17 July 1922, 7, https://paperspast.natlib.govt.nz/newspapers/AS19220717.2.99

166 *Auckland Star*, 22 July 1922, 12, https://paperspast.natlib.govt.nz/newspapers/AS19220722.2.129

168 Courtesy Nirder Singh

170 Courtesy Nayna Bhana

173 Courtesy Lalita Hari

175 Alexander Turnbull Library, Ref: WA-12555-G

176 Alexander Turnbull Library, Ref: N-P-2194-5., *Evening Post*, 11 April 1914, 5, https://paperspast.natlib.govt.nz/newspapers/EP19140411.2.34

176 Alexander Turnbull Library, Ref: N-P-2191-8., *New Zealand Herald*, 7 August 1929, 8, https://paperspast.natlib.govt.nz/newspapers/NZH19290807.2.20

183 Courtesy Chris Sullivan, photographer

185 Sample media headlines reproduced from: *Otago Daily Times*, 20 September 2019; *Indian Weekender*,13 January 2014; *New Zealand Herald*, 5 June 2019; *Otago Daily Times*, 15 January 2020; *New Zealand Herald*, 17 June 2018; *Indian Weekender*, 27 February 2017; *NZH*, 10 August 2019; *Hawke's Bay Today*, 3 Sept. 2012; *Horowhenua Chronicle*, 7 August 2019; *Indian Weekender 16 May 2019; New Zealand Herald*, 3 January 2014*; New Zealand Herald* 19 July 2018*; Otago Daily Times*, 24 November 2011; *Indian Weekender*, 7 November 2019; *Newshub*, 29 February 2020

191 Courtesy *Metro* (NZ), October 1994

194 *New Zealand Herald*

196 Photograph by Narendra Badekar. Courtesy *Indian Newslink*

196 *Ouellette Gazette*, 20 October 2010. Courtesy Edwin Ouellette, illustrator

201 *Stuff* Limited

209 Courtesy New Zealand Human Rights Commission

210 Courtesy Paul Williams, *Horowhenua Chronicle*

Acknowledgements

My most heartfelt thanks go to Manisha Morar, General Secretary of the New Zealand Indian Central Association (NZICA) for convincing me to return to the roots of my academic research — and my outrage about racism in Aotearoa New Zealand — to document the discrimination that Kiwi-Indians have faced. I was invited to develop a document outlining Kiwi-Indians' grievances that Nigel Murphy had compiled in 2007.

When compiling my document for NZICA, I was galvanized to record, not just overt racism against Kiwi-Indians, but also the more subtle ways in which Kiwi-Indian invisibility is part of Aotearoa's history of discrimination and exclusion. With the support of Nicola Legat and Massey University Press, we have produced this book. NZICA, President Paul Patel and Manisha Morar have been behind this project and I sincerely thank them, and the many Kiwi-Indians who have made such research possible.

I also acknowledge those who have supplied information and advice, for this publication, especially the late Hew McLeod, and Craig Giddens, Michael Roche, Abdullah Drury, David Littlewood, Jared Davidson, Swaroopa Prameela Unni, Vasanti Unka and my dear partner Graham Boyle. Wonderful support has also come from Pinky Agnew, Savita Kerry and Bee Dawson. Many thanks to the staff of Archives New Zealand, the National Library of New Zealand, and the Hocken Collections at the University of Otago.

Massey University Press has been a delight to work with, especially Tracey Borgfeldt but also Anna Bowbyes, Matt Turner and Olive Owens.

I am most grateful to Professor Kate Hunter and Associate Professor Anna Green at the Stout Centre for New Zealand Studies, Victoria University of Wellington, and Professor Cathy Coleborne at the University of Newcastle in Australia for enabling my institutional support during the writing of this book.

About the Author

Jacqueline Leckie is a researcher and writer based in Ōtepoti Dunedin. She was a former J. D. Stout Research Fellow and is now an adjunct research fellow with the Stout Centre for New Zealand Studies at Victoria University of Wellington, and conjoint associate professor in the School of Humanities and Social Sciences at the University of Newcastle. She is a fellow of the New Zealand Indian Research Institute, and an affiliated researcher of Centre for Global Migrations (Otago). Her research has concerned the Indian diaspora, development, gender, ethnicity, mental health and work within the Asia–Pacific. She taught at the University of the South Pacific, Kenyatta University and for 27 years at the University of Otago. Her books include *Indian Settlers: The Story of a New Zealand South Asian Community* (2007), *To Labour with the State* (1997), *Colonizing Madness: Asylum and Community in Fiji* (2020), and *A University for the Pacific: 50 Years of USP* (2018).

Jacqui can be contacted on jacquileckie123@gmail.com

Index

Bold page numbers indicate photographs and illustrations.

F

G

H

I

N

O

P

Q

R

S

T

U

V

W

Y

First published in 2021 by Massey University Press
Private Bag 102904, North Shore Mail Centre
Auckland 0745, New Zealand
www.masseypress.ac.nz

Design by Sarah Elworthy

A catalogue record for this book is available from the National Library of New Zealand

Printed and bound in Singapore by Markono

ISBN:978-0-9951407-2-1
eISBN:978-0-9951465-3-2

The publisher thanks the New Zealand Indian Central Association
for their support in making this publication possible